the
Joy of
Gardening

Dedication
For my dear old Uncle Albert

the Joy of Gardening

THE EVERYDAY ZEN OF MOWING THE LAWN

Ellen Mary

greenfinch

Contents

Introduction

When you discover the joy of gardening, rather than seeing it as a collection of jobs that 'have' to be done – such as mowing the lawn – you will unquestionably start to feel your connection with the planet and understand how all living beings are closely intertwined in a web of wonder, interdependent on each other for survival.

I learned this over many years of gardening, but it was some time before I realized how essential gardening is to overall wellbeing – until there was time in my life when I needed it the most. I began to recognise that as I worked on my allotment and in my garden, my mind was at ease with everything happening in my life. Each flower that I nurtured became a friend – the type who you can always rely on to bring a smile to your face – and each vegetable grown from a tiny seed in my hand gave an enormous sense of satisfaction that I couldn't find at the time in anything else I was trying to pursue. Even the total exhaustion after a day of heavy-duty gardening became a welcome feeling and as I allowed myself to rest, replenishing my body with food made from plants I had grown was a deliciously empowering experience.

Following this realization, I decided to find out why gardening made me feel at peace with the world, why it helped me to reset at the end of each day, and ultimately why being in the garden makes such a big difference to so many people around the world – not just socially and economically but also physically and emotionally.

When I was a child, I truly believed that fairies lived at the end of our garden. We grew fruit and vegetables in front of the shed and I used to sit on the step and imagine I could see a family of fairies enjoying the gooseberries and peas as much as I did. It was pure escapism, full of whimsical dreams of magic happening in the kitchen garden. What I didn't realize then, but I do now, is that I didn't have to imagine magic happening because it's already there all around us – up in the sky, in the trees, as each flower blooms and in the mind-blowing world beneath the soil, and most importantly, in our deep connection to it all. My journey of finding joy through gardening started in that kitchen garden, and I hope you will follow a similar journey of happiness as you read this book.

Over the years I have studied the practice of horticulture, social and therapeutic horticulture, and cognitive behaviour therapy; I have worked as a gardener, met some of my most treasured friends through gardening and realized the importance of spreading the word about nature as an intrinsic link to our wellbeing. I never expected to appear on television or radio, or to write a book, but you never know where your path will take you when you find your passion! With this book as a guide, I hope you will embark on a way of life that encompasses self-care through plants and nature. This may well bring you the clarity you need to pursue your own passion.

It can be difficult to balance the stresses of modern life with time engaging with the natural world, but this simple practice can provide immense benefits, so in this book you'll find many quick and easy tips for finding time for gardening, cooking and being creative – allowing you the space to find harmony among a busy life.

Gardening and growing your own food is enlightening and will help you to feel hope, responsibility and so much joy. As you embark on your own gardening journey, remind yourself that gardening is a mixture of education, exploration and practical work, but also an act of self care for your physical and mental health wellbeing. When you find a balance between the two, you will truly thrive in all aspects of gardening and discover how it can positively influence your life.

The wellbeing tips provided in the pages of this book are all activities that I practise myself as I garden, and will prompt you to pause for important moments of observation, rest and reflection, during which you can appreciate a deep joy of nature. The practical advice will help you to approach gardening holistically – after all, everything you do creates an impact, and in the garden that impact reaches every part of your mind, body and soul.

Gardening can create a better world, not just for you but for every living being on this big, beautiful planet. Let your journey begin.

Planning your Garden

Whether a balcony or large plot, the experience of evolving with your garden is one of the greatest joys of a gardener. Enjoy the excitement as you start to visualize what lies ahead for your space. To get the most from your garden and plant sustainably for the future, it's every bit in the planning as the planting. Many of these principles apply to other areas in our life as well, if only we let them. In the planning of your plot, be it designing from scratch or simply choosing which bulbs to plant for next year, you are identifying your needs and desires, setting goals and aspirations, and putting practical plans in place – all essential tools for personal wellbeing.

The Patient Approach to Gardening

Maybe you have decided to spruce up your space or perhaps you have moved into a new home; there are so many reasons for shaking up a garden, patio or balcony, not least because you want to take on this incredible journey to better connect with the natural world. It can be exciting to hurry into buying plants, but all good things really do come to those who plan first. Consider the planning process to be the start of a lifelong relationship, an ever-evolving project where you will feel connected, enthused and in tune with your garden. Working with nature, from the weather to the soil and the wildlife around you, is one of the most rewarding ways to uplift the mind and will be far more successful than working against the elements.

The start of your own garden journey is an exhilarating time: you will learn new skills, lift your senses in the most beautifully holistic of ways and immerse yourself in the natural world right there at home. Accept that allowing yourself the time to be creative with planning can be incredibly empowering.

In order to make the most of your space it is important to plan properly. This chapter will take you through four stages of planning: observing your space, visualizing your ideal garden, sketching plans and choosing plants.

The very first thing to remember is that patience really is a skill that will bring you enormous rewards as you watch your garden through the seasons. And planning, as with gardening in general, starts with patience.

Getting to Know Your Garden

One of the most important aspects of planning is the practice of observing what is happening in your garden already. There are many things in your garden that you may have never noticed before, from individual blades of grass to bugs under stones. There are cracks in brickwork and different plants each month. New bulbs may emerge in spring and during summer your garden might be a riot of colour until winter when snow covers the grass. There will be a change in bird song at various times throughout the year and the sun will shine in different places as the seasons change. Every day you will see something new, even if you think you have already seen it all. There is always something to spot if you take the time to pay attention. Be in the moment and listen, watch and learn.

If you can find the patience to observe and document each season for a whole year you will gain a thorough understanding of what is already in place in your garden. It's very easy to accidentally dig up something you might really love if you get stuck in too soon or to choose plants that may not thrive. A whole year of patience of course isn't everyone's cup of tea and if you feel like now is the time and you want to seize the day, then observe as much as you can before you start planning any changes.

Visualizing Your Space

When you are ready to get started, creative visualization is a wonderful technique to use to plan out your garden. At the same time your body will become calmer and more relaxed as you enjoy painting a picture of the shapes, structures, trees, shrubs, plants and imagine the pleasure you will get from the garden. Use the following steps as prompts for your visualization. This is best done over a couple of weeks to build up the picture fully, filling in all the details and becoming comfortable and familiar with the space you wish to create.

Firstly, imagine how you want your garden to look.
Just taking the time to build up layers of images in your mind is a relaxing and therapeutic exercise in itself and this technique can be used for many goals you have in life.

Imagine the plants, colours, fragrance, even feel the breeze and the sun on your face. Have you seen images you love of plants you would like to grow? Are there specific birds you would like to encourage into your haven? Can you taste the edible plants you want to use in cooking? Use your mind's eye to build a picture and allow all of your senses to be stimulated in your visualization. Feel what it is like to be gardening, laughing with friends, the kids running around on the lawn or reading a book on your own. As your garden comes together in your mind, look closely at specific details. How tall are the plants? What pots might you grow in? Will there be clover in the lawn (perhaps even a four-leaf clover)? It can be as fun or tranquil as you like. This practice allows you to feel positive emotions and pictures that bring you joy, and it also allows your brain time to switch off from a busy world, which can in turn ease anxiety and stress.

Remember that all gardens evolve; this will help you to visualize how you anticipate your garden to be. There will be times you might decide to move pots and furniture, change plants and add something new to your space. This is a beneficial thought to hold with you as you imagine your ideal. It's completely natural to have a goal and, as you work towards it, decide to take a different route or desire something else. This is all about discovering yourself and what you would like to achieve on your personal journey. Sometimes we have to start the journey to work out where we are going. There may be bumps and turns on the road that you didn't anticipate along the way but you can work with them and continuously learn, evolve and develop yourself as you navigate through life.

Take some time to watch wildlife so that you can visualize a garden that works with nature. Wake up early some mornings and step into your garden while listening to the birds or watching the insects, and breathe in deeply as you scan each plant, each leaf, each drop of morning dew. Stand on the lawn, if you have one, and allow yourself to feel connected to the Earth. Under the surface there is much activity, from worms breaking down the soil to the many millions of good bacteria working hard at encouraging biodiversity in your garden. There is no better place to have a positive impact on wildlife than in your own garden. When you start to recognize the wildlife already enjoying your space, add them into your visualization, enjoying the plants you have provided as food and shrubs for protection. Keep building the picture

Creating an inspiration board

Inspiration boards can be used for anything in life that you would like to achieve. It's a way of expressing your visualization on paper and adding some clarity to your goals. You can build your board in any way, from scrapbook-style to a cork board with pins or using some cardboard and glue. You can add any diagrams or images, written words, colours, plant cuttings, examples of gardens you've seen, photos of wildlife, even feathers, pine cones and twigs. This is your inspiration board for your garden, so fill it with your own personal vision.

What is important to you?
Start with the key elements to the design that are essential to you in your garden. These don't have to be practical – this is when you can work with your emotions. How do you want your garden to make you feel? Think of colours to suit that feeling. Go with how you feel first and, as you put more information on your board, enjoy the textures of different materials such as magazine cut-outs, fabrics and natural materials gathered from your garden.

Written word
Affirmations and quotes can add to the inspiration. Add cut-outs of quotes about plants, gardening and anything that helps you to feel good about what you are going to achieve to the board. It doesn't have to be perfect; it's a place for your ideas and creativity to stimulate your mind and help you reach your gardening goals.

in your mind as the garden matures and birds, bees and butterflies share the space with you.

If you have a small garden or a balcony, this process of visualization and planning is no less important. Every single plant will have an impact, perhaps even more so in a limited space. So, consider which pots and small trees may work and how much you will enjoy welcoming beneficial wildlife to your little haven.

When you have created your garden in your mind, continuously nurture your goal by practising this visualization each day and you will feel inspired, excited, even empowered, and ready to make your garden into the sanctuary you want it to be. These moments of time out will also help you to feel calm and peace, which will enhance your wellbeing. Then, when you are completely happy with the full visualization in your mind, it's time to create an inspiration board and put your ideas on paper.

Sketching Garden Plans

Nature is definitely the best artist, providing the finest landscape art to be admired. From the patterns on petals to the colours and shapes in the sky during sunset, there is beauty all around us. Everywhere you turn in your garden there is a piece of art waiting to happen.

Sketching your garden plans doesn't need to be like the work of a professional. You might really enjoy the process and be inspired to take up an art or design class but if putting pencil to paper isn't your thing, think about this stage as the more practical step after visualization. Your lines don't need to be perfect, but it is an important transition before you start to get your hands dirty in the soil. You can use a pen, pencil or crayon – it's entirely your choice. Pencils, however, are ideal for being able to easily make changes as you work on your plans and an eraser will prove very handy!

Your sketches can be as detailed or abstract as you would like. The process is about starting to see how the elements in your visualization will come together and putting your initial thoughts into a rough or concise plan that can help you to bring your ideas to life. You can refer to it, change it and be guided by it as you get to work in your garden.

Remember as you sketch, to look over your inspiration board (see page 17) and bring to mind your previous visualizations. Recall the feeling, the emotion, colours and structures as you move one step closer to shaping your haven.

As your pencil moves on the paper, take pride in the progress you are making and feel the excitement as you see your ideas coming together. At times in life, it's important to take moments to recognize how far you have come. It is all too easy in our busy day-to-day lives to forget our achievements and fail to recognize progress. As you sketch, accept that your own life journey has already come so very far. It will continue in stages and, as you meet hurdles along the track, you will jump over them

or walk around them. Each stage brings with it new learning, enlightenment and the ability to continue moving forwards in the direction you are aiming for.

If you would like to measure your garden, be as precise as you can; start with the overall size and then add in the permanent structures that you won't be moving, perhaps your shed or greenhouse. Next, start to place any hard landscaping such as new patios or pathways. If you are just creating new planting, draw everything you already have in place, leaving room for you to include your new borders or plants next. If you are gardening on a patio or balcony, sketching how you will place your pots – including the heights, colours and where the sun will be – is a great way to pull the picture together.

Detailed Sketches

If you are preparing a new flower bed, you may not need to go into huge detail but it can still be helpful to draw out the size and shape, and draw in circles or shapes where you will place your plants. This allows you the opportunity to see how much space you have and if you can fit in all of the plants you have visualized. You can switch them around until you are happy with the plan before you start to plant out. Think about the eventual size of the plant and draw your shapes to represent this. For example, a hydrangea that may grow to 100cm (3ft) wide would be shown as a larger shape on your plan than a lavender that might only grow to 50cm (1½ft) wide, regardless of the initial size when you first plant them out.

For a more detailed plan, start by measuring your garden boundaries and plot them onto your paper. If you want to draw plans up like a pro, use graph paper and draw to scale and also add in your house dimensions, or at least the rear where it meets the garden. Also note electricity, water, other utilities and anything else you can think of that may impact how you use the space.

To make multiple changes you can use an eraser or use tracing paper. Just place the tracing paper on top of your plan and draw your elements as many times as you like until you are happy your plan is final.

If you would like your plan to be an abundance of colour, representing how your garden will look and feel, use coloured pencils to fill each space. As well as plant colours, it can be helpful to colour-code your utilities, for example blue for water and red for electricity.

*A*bstract Plans

If you decide to sketch your plans in an abstract style, consider mostly how the garden will make you feel. In this style, you are not drawing a specific garden plan but instead allowing yourself to explore colour and shapes, textures and form in any way that feels natural when you put paint to paper. An abstract approach is about creativity, emotion and uniqueness. Your abstract art can be whatever you want it to be and allows great expression. As you draw, permit freedom within your mind but always with your garden as inspiration to run wild on paper.

Any Which Way You Like

Drawing is a personal activity and you could even merge the two styles together or do both. Rough sketching with ideas and words can work really well, still helping to put your thoughts into the shape of your garden and for you to be able to see how things will come together when you start working outside. Add colour, use paint or stick to pencil. This is your plan, your garden and your journey.

Remember no one needs to see your sketches if you don't want them to. You will know when, or even if, you are ready to share your plans.

Soil Life for Connectivity

In modern life we can find ourselves feeling out of touch with the natural environment but, by spending time in a garden, it's easy to discover a deep connection with life on Earth and it all starts with the soil just beneath your feet.

When you understand what a plant needs to flourish, you can begin to appreciate all the intricacies and

connectivity between the Earth and everything around you. This holistic understanding can provide an enormous sense of purpose and appreciation of how everything within the garden is linked – and that includes you.

For plants to truly thrive we need to get to know what helps them to grow. The foundation of most garden plants is the fascinating mix of broken-down rocks, organic material, living organisms, air, water and mineral particles that all work together to make the soil that you plant in. When you touch the soil, you are coming into contact with the very planet that we live on, and the Earthing Theory (the concept of transferring the Earth's energy to the body through contact with the Earth) has shown how this simple action has huge benefits, helping to bring your body into balance.[1] Not only that, but there are many beneficial organisms that you'll make contact with as you touch the soil with your hands, such as microbes called *Mycobacterium vaccae* that can stimulate serotonin production, which in turn helps us to feel relaxed and happy – in effect acting as an antidepressant. [2]

Soil also provides essential habitats for numerous organisms: fascinating fungi, bacteria, insects and wildlife. It is vital to life on Earth. Did you know there are more living organisms in a handful of soil than humans on Earth? It might not look pretty, but it's what's beneath the surface that counts.

There are different types of soil, depending on your geograpical location, and understanding which type you have in your garden can help you to choose the best plants to grow. Each scoop of soil is like a fingerprint (see Identifying Your Soil Type on page 30), allowing you to assess and identify its charateristics before you begin to plant.

Soil Care

Composting is part of the natural cycle in your garden. It adds beneficial organisms to your soil, reduces waste and is satisfying to make. It's so easy to do – after allowing time for your compost pile to break down, it will replenish your soil naturally – plus it's free! If you have lots of space, making an area just for compost can be really useful but for smaller spaces there are bins that can be used, even on a balcony. Compost needs just a few elements from your kitchen and garden: you can throw in your vegetable scraps, cardboard and newspaper, grass cuttings, twigs, old plants, leaves and much more. To create a good compost, you will need a balance of these elements and not too much of any one material. Give the compost pile a turn every now and again with a garden fork and your perfect organic matter will be ready to nourish your soil from three months onwards.

Fallen leaves provide another way to condition your soil and make a really easy mulch for your plants. As leaves float to the ground during the cooler months of the year, it is actually nature's own way of replenishing the soil. Collect the leaves, place them in a black plastic sack, tie it up and punch some holes in for air, then leave in a safe place until the following year. When you open up the bag, you will find the most wonderful, natural leaf mulch to dig in around your garden plants (see Feeding Plants for Health on pages 94-5).

By creating a healthy soil, not only will your flowers bloom and your vegetables taste delicious, but you will also be contributing to the evolution of life on Earth. Yes, right there, just under your feet. Next time you are out in your garden, why not try taking your shoes off? Feel the natural, negative charge from the core of the Earth, helping to relax you and bring your mind, body and soul into balance.

You don't have to let the complexities of soil baffle you, just know that touching it, working with it, planting in it and looking after it will mean your garden plants will thrive and you will feel an enormous sense of understanding and connectivity by being part of the planetary cycle.

Choosing Your Garden Plants

Deciding which plants are perfect for your garden is one of the most exciting stages – now is the time to action your plans and literally bring your garden to life. Not only will the plants you choose improve the broader environment, but they will also be there to stimulate your own physical and mental health wellbeing.

Shopping for plants online is useful and convenient, with the thrill of anticipation as the package arrives, but if you are able to take the time to visit your local nursery it will allow you the opportunity to get up close to the plants you choose before buying. The wealth of options available can be overwhelming; use the following tips for a more mindful approach to buying plants.

For each plant that you are drawn to, study it with intention. Contemplate closely the form, shape, colours, patterns and textures on each petal and leaf. Consider the emotion that each plant provokes within you.

Visualize the plant in the overall picture of your garden. As you learn about the vast planting opportunities for your garden, your visualization will evolve, which is all part of the process of gardening for wellbeing. You may find plants that you are drawn to but that don't quite fit into your bigger picture, and you will need to decide if you want to adapt your vision or stick to your plan. Perhaps you would like to step out of your boundaries and give something new a try. Or there may be a plant that isn't ideally suited to your garden even though you love it, in which case you will need to decide if it's worth putting energy into attempting to grow it or if it will be better to let it go and find something that will work better. Know that, with each decision, you are building confidence and self-esteem in working towards fulfilling your ambition.

Identifying your soil type

To make sure you choose plants that will thrive in your space you will need to assess the soil type. Before you start planting, get some water and put your hands in the soil. Remember as you do this, how much life there is in that handful and how having this contact is so good for you. Feel the soil between your fingers, then add a little water and try to roll it into a ball. Observe the texture closely – the following guide will help you identify the type:

- **Loam** is the soil all gardeners strive for! It will roll into a ball but it won't be sticky like clay.
- **Clay soil** is sticky, smooth and will roll into a ball.
- **Sandy soil** drains well but can dry out quickly. Rolled in your hands, the soil will crumble away with ease.
- **Peat** is acidic and often found in gardens. It looks dark and is spongy when you squeeze it in your hands.
- **Chalk soil** is alkaline and will visibly have white stony chalk when you collect your sample.

Soil acidity

Most plants will grow in neutral to alkaline conditions but there are plenty of plants that thrive in acidic soil. If you've planted rhododendrons and azaleas and wondered why they haven't grown, it is because they love acidic soil. The easiest way to find out the acidity of your soil is to buy a test kit online. They are cheap, plus it's fun to get scientific in the garden!

As well as making sure the plants you choose fit into your overall plan for your space, there are a number of practical considerations to keep in mind, such as seasonal planting for year-round interest and the growing conditions that each plant requires.

All-year Interest

Each season sees exquisite transformations in the garden. From the new shoots of hope in spring and lush greens in summer to seductive tones in autumn and sleeping plants in winter. Every month you will see something new and, by observing the changes closely, you will learn to appreciate how nature works. A great way to observe the seasons in the garden and to provide an all-year home for wildlife is to ensure there is something growing every month. This is equally easy to do in pots and containers as it is beds and borders.

Choose a variety of *spring* bulbs for a burst of colour to lift your mood when you spot signs of new shoots. If you plant these in autumn you can even create a 'bulb lasagne' in a pot and enjoy them all blooming at various stages in one pot throughout the season.

A bulb lasagne is planting multiple bulbs in layers from bottom to top: start with tulips at the bottom, then daffodils in the middle and lastly crocus as the top layer. If you have room in a large pot you can even add in a couple of hyacinths and some snowdrop bulbs. Hyacinths can be planted in the lower layers and snowdrops towards the top, about 5cm (2in) below the soil.

Summer will see many vegetables and salads, herbs and flowers in bloom. Be dazzled by a cheerful African daisy (*Osteospermum*) and sunny daylilies (*Hemerocallis*) or perhaps swathes of white, frothy false goat's beard (*Astilbe*) and cool, unfurling ferns – true marvels of nature. With endless options, you can fill your garden borders and pots with many plants that you love.

Autumn is full of berries, both stunning to look at and perfect food for wildlife as they store energy for the colder months ahead. Firethorn (*Pyracantha*) is a great hedging plant, producing masses of colourful berries after flowering. Ivy (*Hedera*) is an essential source of food and shelter for birds and can also be great for privacy screening when kept in shape, so it doesn't get unruly.

There may be bare trees in **winter** but there are also plants such as the Christmas rose (*Helleborus niger*), snowdrops (*Galanthus*) and heathers (*Calluna*) to provide you with colour even during the duller days. Winter jasmine (*Jasminum nudiflorum*) and witch hazel (*Hamamelis*) are fragrant additions to the winter garden. If you have space, rowan (*Sorbus*) has clusters of bright berries, starting in the autumn into early winter, that birds love.

We crave greenery all year and the garden can look a little sad if everything is deciduous and drops its leaves in autumn, leaving the bare branches exposed to the elements. But deciduous trees and shrubs have their own beauty to admire. Without them, we wouldn't be able to enjoy the changing autumnal tones and make the leaf mulch required to replenish the soil.

Steadfast evergreens will of course provide year-round interest, shelter and food for birds and other insects, plus gazing out of the window at snow on evergreen shrubs in winter is comforting in itself. Holly (*Ilex aquifolium*) is a well-known UK evergreen that can easily be grown as a bush or hedge. Christmas berry (*Photinia*) is another popular evergreen that is particularly easy to grow and if unpruned will bloom full of white flowers in early summer.

Allow yourself the time to research what can give you year-round interest. It can be quite the tonic to admire garden photographs and find plant inspiration to influence your own garden designs.

Sun and Shade

Each of us has different needs to thrive and be content, and the same is true of plants. Various plants require different growing conditions; some will thrive in shade while others need plenty of sun. To minimize cost and heartbreak, try to choose each plant for the perfect spot. Plant labels and seed packet instructions will say if the preference is sun or shade. Here is a quick guide:

Full sun means at least six hours of direct sunlight on most days. There are very many plants that thrive in full sun.

Part shade means at least three hours of sunlight a day. You will notice the labels of many plants will say that they are sun-loving but can also tolerate part shade.

Shade is less than three hours of sunlight a day with perhaps some dappled sunlight at other times. Never feel restricted if you have a shady garden. Some of the most calming gardens are full of shade-loving plants.

Colour and Form

The colours you choose will have a deep impact on the emotions your garden will arouse. In your visualization and sketches, did you imagine a cool, peaceful colour scheme or is your garden going to excite you with vibrant hot colours?

If dreaming of far-off shores, you may look at a coastal theme with soft greens and hues of blue, growing in borders shaped in soft curves reminiscent of those distant shorelines. For a relaxing haven, various shades of green with accents of white will induce calm as you absorb the softness of nature. For a fiesta, try energetic colours and various textures dancing in pots with jazzy pinks, ostentatious oranges and showy yellows.

Remember your garden is about you and your personality; it can be whatever you want it to be.

Assessing your aspect for perfect planting

An important part of getting to know your garden is understanding the aspect; this is the direction that your garden faces when you look out onto it. The aspect will affect where in your garden the sun shines and the shade rests. There may be sun in one patch in the morning but not during the afternoon and vice versa. You might have a sun trap or a garden in complete shade. Knowing your garden's aspect can help you decide on the right plants, relaxation areas and plan pathways and structures.

North, south, east or west

The quickest way to find out what way your garden faces is to stand at the back of your house (or the front of your house, if you are designing the front garden) with a compass and check to see which way you are facing. If you would prefer to follow the sun, step into the garden at sunrise and sunset to watch where the sun is in the sky. Jot your findings down on a piece of paper.

Where is the sun?

Keep a piece of paper and pencil by your window and each hour of the day draw a line where the sun shines on your garden. This can give you a rough sketch at different times of the day so you can see where there is sun and shade. You can even do this for each season in the garden to see how the sun moves over your space all year.

The 'Rules'

'Right plant right place' is undoubtedly the way to growing a thriving, biodiverse and sustainable garden but sometimes step out of the box and plant what you like even if the theory doesn't say it will work. It's how we learn; your experiment might work or it might not but you will have enjoyed trying! Sometimes taking risks paves the way for the progress you need, plus trial and error is a great way to learn new approaches to life.

DRY GARDEN PLANTS Dry gardens are becoming more important due to the changing climate. Choosing plants for a thriving drought-tolerant garden is ideal for hot, dry gardens and if you have little time to water. Often drought-resistant plants have thick leaves, sometimes glossy or even 'fuzzy', as this all helps them to save water. Try growing agave and *Verbena bonariensis*. Russian sage (*Perovskia*) and euphorbias work well together as do sedums (see illustration, right), foxtail lilies (*Eremurus*) and agapanthus (see illustration, left). Enjoy the shocking colours of red-hot poker (*Kniphofia*) and spiky foliage of eryngium.

Creating
the Sensory
Garden

**One of the most wonderful aspects of gardening is
the awakening of your senses** at any given moment
as you step into and through your garden – from the
cool morning dew on your bare feet to the alluring
fragrance of plants by your patio door. Gardens can be a
place to hide away when you need to or to enjoy fun,
active times with friends and family. Your garden is your
personal space; you can add your own personality and
creativity into your design. It doesn't matter if the
area you garden is small, it is yours to work with and you
can discover so much about yourself as you enjoy creating
a sensory garden, even if simply with pots and window
boxes in a small space.

When you create a sensory garden think about how
you can stimulate all of your senses – touch, smell, sight,
sound and taste. To achieve a full multi-sensory garden
consider at the planning stage how it will be used. Use the
creative visualization technique (see Visualizing Your
Space, pages 14–18) to design your perfect sensory

experience, paying close attention to your emotions when conceptualizing the space.

When planning a sensory garden, emotions are a key consideration as they help to stimulate the senses. Have you enjoyed an experience in the past that a specific plant reminds you of? Do you have emotions attached to plants, such as a flower you had in your wedding bouquet or perhaps your grandparent's favourite blooms? Allow yourself to take a trip down memory lane. Does the smell of roses remind you of your most-loved perfume? Keep in mind these memories when you plan your sensory feast.

Touch

Many plants have the most incredibly interesting textures. These plants are particularly tactile to touch:

Moss is easy to grow, and looks great in any garden or in pots. Feel that spongy moss as you gently apply some pressure with your hands and let it spring back up.

Lamb's ear (*Stachys byzantina*) has a velvety foliage. You'll feel yourself relaxing as you stroke it between your fingers.

Pussy willow (*Salix discolor*) has furry catkins, fluffy and velvety all in one to touch (see illustration, left).

Alliums with their mainly round flower heads that are made up of lots of flowers, are often star shaped and tantalizing to gently touch.

Tibetan cherry (*Prunus serrula*) with its shiny reddish bark has flowers in spring and wonderful all-year-round interest. It is incredibly tactile and leaves a gorgeous effect as the bark peels off the trunk.

Smell

Choose plants that will relax or invigorate your mind as you brush by, crush leaves in your hands or lean in to absorb the fragrance. Some may need to be rubbed to release the oils and the smell will linger on your hands. Herbs may feature widely in a sensory garden for their various aromas. Scents from your garden can be extremely emotive.

Sweet pea (*Lathyrus odoratus*) is perhaps one of the most well-loved fragrant plants among gardeners. As an annual, it erupts into bloom for summer, when you can pick a posy for that classic summery perfume, which never fails to make you smile.

Curry plant (*Helichrysum italicum*) smells exactly like curry, as you might imagine. It has silvery foliage and bright yellow flowers that insects love. The stunning, strong fragrance can't be mistaken from metres away and might even make you feel hungry.

Star jasmine (*Trachelospermum jasminoides*) is a climber full of star-shaped white flowers with a deliciously sweet vanilla fragrance. Perfect for screening fences and for growing by windows and doors to allow the scent to waft in and be inhaled.

Tobacco plant (*Nicotiana*) has an intoxicating sweet smell as the evening draws in. As a bedding plant, it's perfect for borders where you can sit close by and relax with the heady scent, or it can be grown in pots.

Scented geraniums (*pelargoniums*) provide aroma varying from mint to rose and lemon when you rub the foliage. They are both easy to grow and edible, so perfect to pop in a cocktail.

Sight

We know that plants can make us feel happy simply by looking at them. But go one step further and choose the colours, heights and structures to intentionally invoke the mood you want to feel when you spend time in your garden. Choosing cool colours or hot colours is purely down to your own decisions for personal taste. Remember no two plants clash if they make you feel good.

Sunflowers (*Helianthus*) are such happy plants. Tall, strong stems with bright yellow, orange or even red flowers (see illustration, opposite). Watching the flowers turn to the sun is joyous and will help you smile just when you need it.

Love-lies-bleeding (*Amaranthus caudatus*) has drooping panicles of reddish flowers that can be show stoppers in a garden border. They will catch your eye as they dangle in the breeze.

Cosmos are easy annuals to grow for an abundance of bright, cheery flowers and feathery foliage. They can fully fill out a border and are a true feast for the eyes.

Strawberry tree (*Arbutus unedo*) is great for a small garden and during autumn you can delight in seeing both red fruits and white flowers at the same time. So, as the temperature cools and the days are shorter, you can still find beauty in your garden.

Swiss chard 'Bright Lights' is an edible you can easily grow in an ornamental border or in the vegetable patch. The brightly coloured stems can be yellow, red, orange and white, which brings a rainbow in edible form.

Sound

Listening to morning bird song is a wonderful way to start the day. By growing plants that insects love you will attract more birds and wake up to the sound of music. You can have a garden full of sounds to inspire, relax and rejuvenate by simply choosing plants specifically for a particular sound that you love. Planting for pollinators means you will relax to the sound of buzzing bees and fluttering butterflies. Many sounds will be from the breeze through the plants as they sway but also the sound as you shake seedheads, pop buds and rub squeaky foliage.

Bamboo rustles in the breeze and creaks when it gets bigger. Feel like you are on a tropical island as you hear the sounds made by the stalks and leaves.

Love-in-a-mist (*Nigella damascena*) not only has an appearance evocative of romance in a misty place but the seed pods rattle as you collect them. They are simply wonderful to look at and listen to as you shake them.

Bee balm (*Monarda*) is a magnet for bees (see illustration, right). The vibrant flowers are both beautiful and flower for a long time throughout the summer. As perennials they will grow each year and you can listen to the bees going about their work as you relax with a herbal tea.

Honesty (*Lunaria*) can be sown during early summer so they flower the following spring. The flowers are purple and complement a shady border but the true interest is the translucent papery seedheads later in the year as they shimmer in the evening light.

Japanese silver grass (*Miscanthus sinensis*) is easy to look after and yet adds real excitement to the garden. There are many grasses you can choose from for small or larger spaces.

Taste

Growing edible plants makes for a truly productive garden that will also provide nutrition and good health. Choose from fruit and vegetables to herbs and edible flowers to garnish salads, decorate cakes, make herbal medicines and enjoy in drinks. Many of our much-loved garden plants are deliciously edible and will be the ultimate feast for your taste buds.

Mint (*Mentha*) is one of the easiest herbs to grow, but ideally in a pot because it is invasive. There are numerous varieties to choose from peppermint to chocolate mint, so you can pinch a leaf or two as you walk past and feel instantly refreshed.

French marigolds (*Tagetes patula*) are cheerful in shades of red, orange and yellow, with a long flowering season and perfect for companion planting (see page 72). The petals are also edible, with a nice punch to the taste buds.

Lilac (*Syringa vulgaris*) will not only make the air smell sweet in late spring but the flowers can be used in baking and food flavouring or popped in a glass of water.

Society garlic (*Tulbaghia violacea*) gives a delicate flavour without leaving the taste or smell in your mouth, plus the little pink flowers are beautiful on tall grey-green stems.

Buzz buttons (*Acmella oleracea*) are tantalizingly fun! Pop one into your mouth and feel a sensation of tingling to numbing that is bound to make you laugh.

Creating the sensory garden isn't just about flowers. It's important to consider hard landscaping materials, from wood to metal, and also what you will walk on, such as gravel under your boots or a tickle on bare feet from a chamomile lawn (see Alternative Lawns, pages 117–19). You could include a calming water feature; even a pond bucket in a small space adds to the sensory experience of the garden as a whole. Build an area that allows your senses to be aroused and become mindfully awakened to the full beauty of mother nature.

Awaken the Senses

To experience a multitude of wellbeing benefits, take some time out to observe your garden. Look closely at your plants, tune in to the sounds you can hear, focus on details and movements, feel the sensations as you touch foliage and relish the taste of edibles on your tongue. Be in the moment – entirely aware of your thoughts and emotions.

We all look around us, but do we really 'see' what is in front of us? We hear the breeze, but are we really 'listening' to the sound? As we're caught up with the distractions of everyday life, it can be an enlightening practice to focus on the natural world. The garden brings a host of opportunities to tune in and connect with nature for wellbeing – to calm, reset and look after yourself. Try this exercise when you step into the garden:

Take five deep breaths. Inhale through your nose and exhale via your mouth. Breathe in for five seconds and exhale for ten seconds. Breathe for longer or more times if that feels natural to you. When you are relaxed, focus in on:

> *Three* things that you can see.
> *Three* things that you hear.
> *Two* things that you touch.
> *Two* things that you can smell.
> *One* thing that you can taste.

Encouraging Biodiversity

It can be overwhelming at times wondering how we can help the environment on an individual basis. One simple way that you can have a positive impact on the planet is by planting with biodiversity in mind. This means you will encourage a diverse range of species which together create an active ecosystem. You can be a true driving force for nature in your own space no matter what size it is. Small changes can have a big impact, which is no different to circumstances in your own life: sometimes when you need a little help, small steps can be the start of a path to enlightenment.

Creating a home for wildlife is one of the most rewarding aspects in gardening. Part of this is learning to love the little creatures that are welcome in your garden. From the excitement of seeing the first bee on your plants to hearing the rustling of a hedgehog, creating a biodiverse garden allows you to connect to the cycle of life right before your very eyes. Remembering that we are part of nature ourselves and that we can choose what kind of impact we want to have on our planet means that connectivity between our being and the garden becomes all the more meaningful.

Many of our garden creatures are useful for controlling garden pests. Birds eat aphids and toads eat slugs; even wasps play a crucial role keeping levels of greenfly and caterpillars under control. Many different elements come together to create an active and vibrant space.

Plants for Pollinators

A truly flourishing garden is a welcome home to all creatures. Bees, hoverflies, wasps, butterflies, beetles, moths, bats, birds, ants and every other insect you can think of. Even the pests!

Encouraging all creatures means your garden will be awash with biodiversity and much of the pest control will be part of the natural cycle. One way to help this is to plant as much as you can with pollinators in mind. They will busily enjoy your plants at the same time as contributing to the cycle of life. Most plant labels will display a bee symbol if it's a plant that pollinators are attracted to, but a general rule is to ensure that you have some blue, purple and violet plants as research has shown that bees prefer these colours.[3] Also look for single-flowered plants which allow easier access to the nectar and pollen than double heads. If you can easily see where the pollen is on a flower, that's a good sign pollinators may be able to as well.

There are many plants suitable for all size gardens that pollinators will love. Consider plants for all seasons from snowdrops and hellebores in winter, crocus and tulips in spring, perennial plants such as *achillea*, *echinacea* and *rudbeckia* in summer to stonecrop sedums, asters and verbena in autumn.

If you have space, climbers and shrubs provide nesting, resting places and food for garden birds and insects. Ivy is a magnet for insects and moths, which in turn provide food for bats that are an essential part of the ecosystem and eat mosquitos and gnats. Honeysuckle and jasmine are gorgeous climbers with fragrance to lift the spirits and are great for pollinators as well.

Trees for Food and Habitat

Trees and shrubs are essential for all native wildlife as shelter and food, but they also add a special feel to a garden. There are many trees for smaller gardens and even containers, so never feel restricted by size (see Small-space Trees, page 194). Some trees, such as beech, guelder rose and dogwoods, can also be grown as a hedge. Trees that produce berries, such as rowan and holly, are particularly important as a source of food.

Homes for Hedgehogs and Toads

Hedgehogs and toads contribute a great deal to the garden, not least by devouring slugs. Building a wildlife pond brings the most immense amount of satisfaction and joy to the garden – you may even find a rare newt appears. If you are short on space, wildlife ponds can be made from just about any watertight container, from old trugs to sealed butler sinks. Fill your container up with rainwater to ensure there are no chemicals present and add a mix of pond plants to keep the water clean and make it look attractive to you and wildlife.

Rigid hornwort (*Ceratophyllum demersum*) is a native oxygenating plant that naturally filters pond water. Deep-water plants, like water lilies (Nymphaeaceae), are able to cope with reduced sunlight as the plant is submerged in the pond and marginal plants, such as lesser spearwort (*Ranunculus flammula*), will give height

and safe places for wildlife to play around the edge of the pond. If you put stones into your pond, it is easy to then place your plants at different levels. Make sure that wildlife can safely get in and out by placing rocks and plants in and around both a ground pond and a bucket pond. Even if you have a small pond bucket on a balcony or patio, it will soon be found by local wildlife. You'll be amazed at what turns up.

Extra Encouragement

Morning bird song is nature's own music, and you can encourage more in your garden by adding nesting boxes, baths and feeders. You'll find plenty of entertainment as you watch birds feeding and bathing close up. Bat boxes and insect hotels are also great projects to get stuck into that provide extra help for these creatures.

As you build your home for wildlife, carefully observe all the bugs around you. The more ladybirds, hoverflies and even wasps you see, the more you can be sure the cycle is working. Every single little creature in your garden contributes to the wider ecosystem.

Watch the changes throughout the seasons and know that a garden with some unruly areas is very likely to be a wildlife haven. Not mowing all of the lawn, keeping piles of wood and leaving seedheads over winter is a great way to encourage insects. Your garden doesn't have to be perfect, it should just be loved by you and those you share it with.

Seeding, Potting and Transplanting

As you move towards your gardening goals, seeds will be sown, plants will need nurturing and hope for the future will be stirred. In this chapter you will learn how to scatter tiny miracles that will take you on a path of hope, understanding and awe. In planting seeds, propagating and transplanting, we are forced to practise patience, not always an easy skill. As each seed bursts into life, your care will ensure it grows strong and flourishes. Simple tasks with big lessons.

Sowing Seeds for Serenity

Gardening is a restorative, therapeutic activity that can be part of your everyday life or something you dip into as and when you like. The more you garden, the more benefit you will find for your mind and body. In a life where stress can take hold, impacting our mental and physical health, gardening is a way to restore the soul and nurture the mind. The act of gardening encourages the release of serotonin and endorphins, the feel-good hormones, and improves mental health, not least because breathing fresh air and spending time outside can help us to sleep better.[4]

One way to benefit from gardening is by sowing seeds. Here the magic of gardening can be felt as you clear noise from your mind and focus in on tiny little pieces of joy, so full of hope for the future. From these small beginnings, grow great things – with a little care and nurturing. It seems a miracle that a giant pumpkin grows from a small seed that is just slipped under a little soil. How can tiny, raggedy seeds produce a superfood such as beetroot or just one small, half moon-shaped seed go on to become the bright yellow and orange, medicinally useful pot marigold (*Calendula*)? The remarkable journey of those seeds starts in your hands. You have the ability to nurture life, bringing you happiness and good health. Before we dive into the practical side of sowing seeds, here are some tips to make the most of this mindful practice.

Before you sow the seeds you have chosen to grow, feel them gently in your hand. Move some carefully between your fingertips and focus on the sensation.

Some seeds are smooth and round, others are flat and silky. There are many different shape and size seeds, each one with its own identity.

As you sow each seed focus in on the moment, imagining what each one will become and what it will encounter during its life in order to grow and flourish. This is good practice as not only will you be relaxing as your mind clears to focus on this one moment in time, but your senses will be stimulated as you touch the seeds and watch them fall into the compost. Many are fragrant as well, just like the plant they will become. Fenugreek and coriander are great examples of seeds with scent.

There are many different ways to sow seeds, dependent on what you are growing, the time of year and the space you have, but understanding the basic principles can help you to get started.

When to Sow Seeds

Always read the seed packet, which should give you all of the information you need. The majority of seeds are sown in spring and early summer, with successional sowing – the means of ensuring there are ongoing harvests throughout the year – every couple of weeks throughout spring and summer. There are seeds that can be sown in summer and autumn for winter and following year harvests as well. If you have a greenhouse, warm windowsill, covered raised bed or propagator you may be able to extend the growing season by sowing earlier and later in the year.

What to Sow Seeds in

There are numerous items you can sow your seeds in. From coir pots to seed trays, modules and pots, with biodegradable and environmentally friendly options becoming more available. You can be as resourceful as you want because you really don't need to purchase any special equipment to sow seeds. Cut out one side of a milk carton, punch holes in the bottom and you have a recycled, ready-made seed tray. Clean old pots that you have bought plants in and re-use them as well. It's satisfying reducing your waste to produce plants for the planet. Trays are great for sowing lots of seeds such as microgreens, pots and modules are useful for sowing seeds individually or just a couple together, such as salads and leafy greens, and root trainers (which are like modules but thin and deep) are especially good for sowing plants that grow long roots such as sweet peas and broad beans.

How to Sow Seeds

You can use seed-sowing compost which will provide the ideal low level of nutrients to encourage germination but if you are unable to get your hands on some, try a multi-purpose, peat-free compost instead. Fill your trays or pots with the compost, leaving a few centimetres (an inch) at the top – so when you water, the compost doesn't spill over the edges – and gently firm it down with your hands or something with a flat surface, such as a wooden block. After you have sown your seeds, sprinkle a light layer of compost on top, unless the seed-packet instructions say

Know your compost

When you begin to sow seeds and pot up plants it's useful to understand the compost that will be the best growing medium for each stage of growth:

- **Seed compost** is low in nutrients and fine in texture so it's easy for roots to form. It can be used for young seedlings but it doesn't have enough nutrients to feed larger plants.

- **Vermiculite** is used for plants that require a moist growing medium and is a mined mineral processed into granules. It can be mixed into compost or used alone to germinate seeds.

- **Perlite** is volcanic glass after heat has been applied and it puffs up into little white balls which are great to mix in with compost for good aeration and drainage. It can also be used for propagating cuttings and keeps the soil dryer than vermiculite.

otherwise – always follow the instructions as different seeds can require different methods. Seeds can take anywhere from just a couple of days to a few weeks to germinate, so don't worry if your seeds haven't sprouted a few days after sowing; the key skill is patience but it's great fun to check every day anyway.

- **Potting compost** has the right level of water retention and nutrients for more established potted plants.

- **Multi-purpose compost** is a mix that is great for pots, hanging baskets and raised beds. As it tends to be a mix between seed and potting compost it can be used in place of both of those as well. Look for peat-free compost to protect the unique habitats of peat bogs.

- **Cocoa coir** is made from the outer layer of a ripe coconut. It's used as 'discs' to germinate individual seeds, as hanging-basket liners and coir blocks, which are placed in water to break up and then mixed with your compost to loosen the soil to help root growth.

- **Ericaceous compost** is for acid-loving plants such as rhododendrons, azaleas and camellias.

Seed-sowing Conditions

Each seed variety will need certain conditions to grow so always check the instructions on the packet. Most need a warm temperature, moisture, air and the right levels of light. It really is extraordinary to think those tiny seeds you are preparing to sow are little lives, waiting to spring into action when you provide them with the right environment. You don't need a greenhouse – a warm windowsill can be the perfect place as long as it's not too hot. As seeds are tiny, use a misting spray to keep the soil damp but not overwatered and ensure plenty of air circulation around them as they grow. Using a misting spray will ensure the water doesn't wash away the seeds or the compost.

Direct Sowing

When the soil has warmed from late spring onwards, some seeds can be sown directly where they will grow outside in pots or borders. Seed packets usually say when the best time is. If you sow when the soil is too cold, your seeds will struggle to germinate, so patience, in all respects with sowing seeds, is needed.

Before you sow, the soil needs to be prepared to provide the best conditions. Remove weeds and rake over the soil to remove any large clumps and stones. Ideally the border needs to be prepared and mulched (see Feeding Plants for Health, pages 94–5) weeks, if not months, before sowing to allow the mulch to break down. You can then rake the soil much finer when you are ready to sow, allowing the seeds better contact with the soil. The soil should be moist but not too wet. A great benefit to sowing direct is learning that there is no rush to get the seeds in the ground. If you run out of room for trays of sown seeds inside early in the year, leave the ones that can be sown directly in the soil until later, allowing you space and time to breathe. Much like your seeds.

The Importance of Labels

It is so easy to forget what you've sown and where, especially if you are growing lots of plants. Labelling is really very useful and fun to do. As you write plant names on ready-made or home-made labels, it will reinforce the name and variety that you are growing in your mind, so you learn plant names as you go. There are reusable labels available but another great way to save waste is to use household items. Use lollipop sticks, paint pebbles, cut up food pots and corks on toothpicks to write plant names on. It's a great way to get creative.

However you decide to sow and grow, relax into the peacefulness of it. The gentle practice of sowing rows in trays or sprinkling them in pots draws your attention towards the now, but as you cover each seed with compost, think about what the future holds for them and for you, as you grow together. It's a wonder to see the first shoots appear but you'll need to continue practising patience as you nurture them to their full potential and remember that some things worth having can take time.

Bulbs, Corms, Tubers and Rhizomes

Plants start their lives under the soil where roots establish, nutrients and water are stored and where they preserve energy over winter so they are ready to burst forth and flower when it's time. What goes on under the soil is quite remarkable and can be seen as very similar to the activity that goes on inside the human body. Inside us there are numerous processes working away at keeping us fit and well, even though we can't see them. Our body and mind need sleep to recuperate, we need fuel to be energized and we need water, light and food to survive and develop – just like plants. Understanding the cycle of growth and where it starts is a key part to feeling connected to the plant life around you. This will ultimately help your plants thrive so you can enjoy them as they grow up through the soil to become something beautiful in your garden.

So, What Exactly are Bulbs, Corms, Tubers and Rhizomes?

Generally, they are all referred to as bulbs but actually each is different, apart from all being planted under the soil where they store nutrients like an energy reserve so they can grow, flower and lie dormant again. You can liken each stage to us throughout the changing seasons. In winter we wrap up warm, put our feet up and stay inside more, just like the bulbs hidden away under the soil. In spring we start to emerge and swap our warm coats for spring jackets, just as the bulbs start to show up and shoots push out of the soil. During summer we thrive as we absorb vitamin D and enjoy the great outdoors at the same time most bulbs are blooming. Then along comes autumn and we start to think about tucking ourselves away again, as the foliage of the flowers dies back for the cycle to start all over again.

Bulbs

Bulbs are made up of many incredible layers of modified leaves which you can see if you cut one in half. They have a sprout in the middle which will become the stem and flowers, with roots at the bottom allowing nutrients and water to be absorbed. Bulbs vary in size from huge amaryllis to tiny snowdrops and include daffodils, tulips and alliums. They will mostly be round or slightly egg-shaped with a flat bottom and a point at the top.

Corms

These look similar to bulbs but tend to be flatter and are actually solid stem bases. As the flowers grow, the nutrients are absorbed so the corm withers away, then energy from the stem and leaves is used to build a new corm and the plant regenerates itself. Gladiolus, crocus and crocosmia are all grown from corms.

Tubers

The most well-known tubers are dahlias and potatoes. Tubers are basically swollen underground stems that can be long or stumpy, slightly round or thin, and they store nutrients for the plants to grow above the soil in a similar way to bulbs and corms. They have 'eyes', which is where the shoots grow from and many are edibles, such as Jerusalem artichoke and sweet potato.

ENCOURAGING REGROWTH Do not cut back the leaves after any bulbs, corms, tubers or rhizomes have finished flowering until they have naturally died off. Leaves need time to produce and store the energy to regrow the following year. Not all bulbs will survive a winter under the soil and some, such as dahlias and tulips, may do better with lifting and storing in a cool, dry place.

Rhizomes

A rhizome is another swollen stem that grows horizontally just below the surface with nodes where stems will shoot up and through the soil. Often they grow so close to the surface that they are visible just under the soil, such as iris and ginger.

We all need to allow ourselves restful times to recharge and re-energize before we rise, refreshed and ready to take on the world. Next time you plant out, look closely at the bulb, corm, tuber or rhizome because, just like those, inside your beautiful body is so much energy, so much goodness, resilience and a little something waiting to bloom.

Finding Hope in New Growth

There is nothing more magical than watching tiny plants burst into life. As your seedlings grow, keep a close eye on each stage of growth – this way you'll get to know every plant and feel a greater sense of connection. Depending on the time of year and the type of plant you are growing, you might be surprised at how fast they develop 'true leaves' – a set of full leaves off the stem. Some seedlings will grow slower and need more time. Either way, they all need to be prepared for the outside world if you are growing them inside before planting out.

Thinning Out Seedlings

As your seedlings become stronger there are a few things you will need to do to ensure they are growing well enough to plant outside. Of course, you might have sown directly into the soil where they are to grow, usually after the soil has warmed up in late spring, but 'thinning out' (also known as 'pricking out') may still apply.

It is likely that you have more than one seedling growing in a pot, tray or module, perhaps in a greenhouse or on a windowsill; when the seedlings are about 3cm (1¼ in) tall and have developed their first set of true leaves, it will be time to create some space for the strongest plants to grow and to allow for better air circulation, which lessens the chance of diseases. This practice is called thinning out. Each plant is given the space, nutrients and light needed for its roots and leaves to grow bigger. Depending on what you are growing, this might not be the only time you thin out before eventually planting out your seedlings in the positions where they will grow into fully mature plants. Some plants will grow bigger and become crowded before the first leaves appear; in this case you can still thin out and pot on without damaging the seedlings. The best practice is to keep an eye on your plants and, if they are getting larger or crowded, it's time for thinning out.

This selective practice gives you, as the gardener, some time to focus and clear your mind of any white noise from outside pressures. We live in a world where multi-tasking is celebrated, even strived for, but we know that focusing on a single task at a time can help to ease stress, increase productivity and get a better job done.[5] Just like sowing seedlings, thinning out can allow you to forget everything else going on. It's just you and your seedlings working together for the future.

Thinning out requires just a few items and your full attention. The process is simply removing the weaker seedlings to make way for the stronger ones to grow. You might decide you don't want to compost the weaker seedlings in which case you can pot them on to provide them with the chance to flourish. Alternatively, many types of edible young seedlings are delicious to eat so just collect, clean and throw on a salad or in a smoothie.

If the compost is light, you may be able to remove seedlings by gently lifting each one, but it is likely they will have rooted well and therefore a little more care will be needed to ensure there is no root damage in the process. You can use a pencil or a small stick, such as a lollipop stick, and if you lightly water the compost first the roots will be easier to lift.

Here are some tips for a more focused and mindful approach to thinning out:

Feel the movement of the roots making their way up through the compost as you gently ease each of the smaller seedlings out with your pencil or stick. Touch the leaves and look closely at the shape, texture and any detail on these tiny little plants. Take deep breaths and concentrate on those small shoots of hope in your hands.

Think of thinning out as decluttering your mind, if you choose to compost or discard any of the seedlings you have removed. Likewise, let go of the things that you don't need in your life – any negativity, anxiety or stress. It can be hard to do but, for each seedling you throw away, let go of a negative thought, a draining person or situation and then focus on the remaining seedlings and nurture them so they continue to grow in strength.

If you are not ready to let go, plant the smaller of the seedlings into another pot, module or tray of compost and see if they too can grow stronger. If they don't improve, remember they can later be removed to make way for stronger things to come. Of course, some will thrive and grow, and that too can create an enormous sense of satisfaction. Whichever way you decide to go, realize and understand that you are doing everything needed to nurture and care for your plants.

When you have removed the weaker seedlings, pat down any disturbed compost around the remaining seedlings, gently water in and give them time to grow on to the next stage. Don't forget to label your seedlings; adding a note on a lollipop stick will do. The best time to thin out is during the morning and evening or on a cloudy day. This means the seedlings are less likely to struggle in the midday heat and sun after their roots have been disturbed. Each one needs a little time to settle in.

Potting on Young Plants

When your seedlings have grown bigger and are more of the size of a plug plant (up to about 8cm/3in in height), many will need potting on to their final growing pot or they may need potting on more than once into increasingly big pots until they are ready to grow to maturity in a larger pot or be transplanted outside. Potting on is the stage of growth when the roots are allowed more space to grow. You'll know when they are ready as their roots will be poking through the bottom of their current pots or modules and they will have grown into much stronger plants.

Some seedlings that you have already thinned out will be ready to go straight to the next stage of hardening off in readiness to transplant outside (see Hardening Off Your Plants, pages 79–80). Plants that prefer to be potted on first include tomatoes, chillies and aubergines. Potting some plants on one more time before they are ready for their final destination can give them the opportunity to establish really good roots. It is also useful if the weather is still too cool to plant them outside and they need more space in the interim.

LESSONS IN GROWTH Like seeds, each of us needs care and we each grow in different ways. It may take time to undertake the journey that you are going on and, as you watch those small plants grow, their transformation can bring you hope for the future in whatever you are aiming for.

Potting on is as easy as these three simple steps:

1. Have your pots ready and fill them with compost, leaving a hole in the middle the size of the rootball of the plants you are potting on. Always leave about 1cm (½in) from the top of the compost to the pot rim to allow for watering.

2. Then carefully remove your plants from their current pots and pop them in the ready-made hole in their new pots. Pat down around the plants and tap the sides of the pots to make sure all gaps are filled with compost.

3. Gently water them and place them in a light position to give them the best chance to grow strong.

Companion Planting

Just as we thrive with companionship, so do plants. As humans, connection with others is part of who we are and can influence who we become. It is one of the most basic needs for us to be happy and healthy, – it deepens our sense of purpose. Companions help to combat loneliness, boost mental stimulation and a network of supportive connection invigorates positive wellbeing. It is important to be around people who look out for you and are there to support you as you grow. Similarly, just like us, not all plants enjoy growing next to each other and, as it is wise to put some distance between yourself and those who have a negative impact on your life, the same applies to plants.

Choose Your Companions Wisely

Plants in the natural world have an astounding ability to know how to work together but there will be times when some plants don't thrive due to incompatible neighbours – if you're growing something tall that is shading or smothering something smaller, for example.

There are a number of plants that are often used for companion planting. The theory is they play two roles: one role is to protect the other plant from pests and perhaps diseases, and the other is purely sacrificial – they are planted with the knowledge that they will most likely succumb to pests in order for the other plant to thrive.

Companion Plants

Marigolds (*Tagetes*) in any garden can repel whitefly and even carrot-root fly, plus the spicy scent attracts pollinators who in turn will eat the aphids.

Nasturtiums (*Tropaeolum majus*) are well known to attract blackfly which keeps them off your other plants. Caterpillars will also have a feast with them, again leaving your other crops alone.

Thyme (*Thymus vulgaris*) has a scent that deters blackfly from your cabbages, not to mention the flowers are highly attractive to bees.

Lavender (*Lavandula angustifolia*) has a strong scent that can confuse pests and deter aphids, plus many insects love it.

Good Combinations

Basil and **tomatoes** not only make great pizza toppings but basil may also help to improve the taste of tomatoes.

Chives and **carrots** are particularly well suited because the scent of the chives is an excellent deterrent to carrot-root fly.

Garlic and **roses** combined are said to be a natural way to prevent black spot and even greenfly.

Borage and **strawberries** (see illustration above) are a common combination and are said to improve both the growth and flavour of strawberries.

Diversity

Ensuring your garden is diverse is by far the best kind of companion planting. This will encourage beneficial insects, better soil health, a host of wildlife, a range of colour and interest, and greater beauty in everything you see.

Work towards planting a wide variety of plants, and use as many native plants as possible, since these work better in their natural environment. However, don't be deterred from trying non-native species as plants often have the ability to work together. Try to plant a mix of evergreen and deciduous shrubs, some trees if you have space and a combination of perennial and annual plants. Keep your eye on how things are progressing and watch the cycle of garden life at its very best as you build a strong environment and a better chance for your garden to thrive.

LIFE LESSONS We can relate companion planting to human companionship: in both you need to ask who you want in your life, who brings you joy and who will fight your corner. Continually likening gardening and plants to what is going on in your own life can be surprisingly revealing and bring to light changes that you may need to make for greater happiness.

TAKE A MINDFUL NOTE As you prepare your plants for their next stage of growth, don't forget to check in with yourself. If you have lots of plants it can seem a daunting and time-consuming task to pot so many on but remember this is a positive step in the right direction to encourage strength within the plant and the roots under the compost. Without taking care of what lies beneath, the plant above the surface won't thrive.

So, as you bring yourself into the moment, check that you are looking after yourself internally to allow your true self to grow in strength. If you have any ideas of how you can better prepare yourself for growth and wellbeing, simply jot them down in a notebook to look back on later and then bring yourself back into the moment. These plants represent hope for the future – they will surprise you, delight you and provide you with a huge sense of achievement over the months to come.

Caring for Young Plants

Gardening is a lifelong learning process so there is no need to think you have to know everything all at once for your garden to thrive. Nature has its own way and you will often find when some things don't grow so well, others will thrive without much care. Many times, you will delight in watching plants grow even in conditions the theory doesn't back up. As you observe your plants through each stage of their lives, you will learn what they need and how they react to different conditions and, as you begin to better understand your garden, also allow yourself your own time and space to grow along with your plants. You need to care and nurture yourself, just like your young plants that will now be ready to grow on to even more beautiful things.

Recognizing that self-care is an essential part of growth is a fundamental step towards a healthy mind and body. Applying self-care when you garden is about taking your thoughts away from everyday stresses to be present in the moment. It is just you and the plants you are caring for. As you observe your plants growing, your sense of optimism will grow alongside them and your confidence will be building too. As each plant develops new leaves and buds waiting to bloom, feel your self-esteem developing because with care, focus and fun, you are able to make great things happen.

Nurturing with Positive Affirmations

Once your seedlings are established, it is time for them to transition to their final planting position. This may require the transitional stage of hardening off (see opposite) before you finally transplant your seedlings into the garden. Before this, take a moment to recognize how you are feeling. We often suppress our thoughts and emotions but allowing time for self-reflection is essential for mental health wellbeing.

You have nurtured your plants to this point and from here they will continue to need support in various ways at different growth stages. What stage are you at? What do you need to reinforce in order to develop and grow?

Set some affirmations that you can say to yourself each day. Try any of the following:

'I can accomplish this'
'I forgive myself'
'I am grateful'
'I believe in myself'
'I am beautiful'
'I am proud of myself'

Positive affirmations can reduce stress, anxiety and help you to overcome difficult times, self-criticism and negative thoughts. They are part of nurturing your wonderful self. Believe in yourself as much as you do your plants.

Hardening Off Your Plants

If you have been growing plants on a warm windowsill or in a greenhouse, as the weather warms up and before they are planted outside, they need to be hardened off. Imagine being all cosy and warm inside your home for weeks and then walking outside with little clothing in cool air and even colder nights. It would be a shock! It's no different for your plants. If you plant them straight outside they will struggle, if not be lost altogether. Hardening off is another stage of the nurturing process, where your plants are given time to adjust. It's a big step towards blooming flowers or delicious fruits and vegetables.

Place your plants, still in their trays, pots or modules, outside during the day and bring them back inside for the

night. Your plants will thank you for easing them in to the outside world. The process should be for about two weeks and towards the end of that time, having checked the weather, you can try leaving them outside overnight as well. Make sure it is not too cold and definitely not frosty. Watch your plants grow and adapt to the change of conditions. The compost will dry out quicker if it is sunny, so keep a check on moisture levels, but don't overwater.

> **ADAPTING TO CHANGE** Much like plants adapting to being outside, when there is change in our lives sometimes we need to learn to adapt and adjust to move forwards with a growth mindset, to flourish in our skin.

Transplanting Out

After a few weeks of acclimatizing to the change of conditions, your plants will be ready to plant out where you would like them to grow. It's important to keep a check on the weather so you know when it's the right time. If it is too cold and there are frosts due, or conversely, if it is too hot and sunny, your seedlings may succumb to the elements. The ideal time to plant out is when the soil is warm in late spring and early summer. Not all seedlings are planted at this time of year so always check your seed packet. However, the majority will be transplanted during this period and not only is it good for them, but for you as well. After winter when spring kicks into action, you can listen to the bird song and absorb some vitamin D on the sunnier days and you'll feel like a hedgehog emerging from hibernation. Springtime is like a tonic for the soul as you get your hands in soil and feel the sun on your back.

Water your plants in their pots before you begin to transplant them. Make sure where they will go has been weeded and the soil is loose (see Ways to Weed, pages 101–2). Use a hand trowel to dig a hole big enough for the plant to go into easily, then remove the plant by gently easing it out of its pot. The roots may be growing through the drainage holes at the bottom and they might be tight to remove. Just tap on the sides and bottom and continue easing them out with as little root disturbance as possible. Don't worry if some of the roots do fall away, they will soon settle into their new home and grow bigger and stronger. Plant it in the pre-dug hole and fill the hole back up with some of the soil that you removed. Tap down the soil around the base of the plant and give it another water.

Protection from the Elements

When you have transplanted them, your plants may need extra protection from the elements. It is good to have a plan in hand should the weather take an unexpected turn and get cold again. The following ideas can easily be put together in a few minutes and will protect your little plants to make sure they continue to grow without problem:

CLOCHES

These are available in many different shapes and sizes, from the classic bell-shaped cloche to a full tunnel. They are a way to protect young plants from the cold, wet and windy weather and from certain pests. Bell-shaped cloches are great for individual plants and can be used on pots, while tunnels can cover rows of plants all in one.

TUNNELS

Great for providing extra protection for your plants, tunnels can be made from metal, wood or plastic. They are just like mini polytunnels and can be found in many different sizes with different coverings, such as net or fleece, and provide extra warmth during cold spells. You will just need to push the hoop ends into the ground ensuring the covering is over all of your plants. As your plants grow strong and the weather is warmer, you can remove the protection and let your plants flourish on.

MAKE YOUR OWN

Part of the gardening fun is being creative and resourceful. Even if you've not dabbled in DIY before, it's good to step out of your comfort zone and see what you can come up with. Plant protection can be made with all kinds of materials that may otherwise get thrown away (see Reusing Household Items in the Garden, pages 84–5). Pieces of plastic can be re-used and made into a shelter for plants and old drinks bottles can have the bottoms cut off and be placed over the plants. Making your own protection adds a personal touch while helping the environment as well.

No-dig gardening

A method of gardening that has gained popularity recently is 'no dig'. It involves barely ever digging soil, if at all, and simply replenishing it with a layer of well-rotted organic compost each year. This method allows the work to be done as nature intended. Worms, fungi and insects, with the help of rain, will work the soil so the nutrients from the compost are absorbed with minimal interference from us.

Make a no-dig bed
There is no need to dig up any weeds unless they are persistent and perennial such as brambles or docks. Cut any taller weeds down and lay cardboard where your bed will be, then cover it over with a thick layer of mulch up to about 5cm (2in) deep. If you have garden beds already cleared of weeds, there is no need for the cardboard – just add a 15cm- (6in-) thick layer of well-rotted organic compost on top of the soil to exclude light from reaching any weeds and seeds.

How to maintain the bed
As you are excluding light and not turning the soil, the seeds within won't get a chance to grow, so you will have far fewer weeds. Use your hoe or hand weed to clear any that appear. Add a layer of mulch about 3–5cm (1¼ –2in) thick each year to replenish the soil and be prepared to be amazed! When you harvest, use a fork rather than a spade and rake the area over, ready for the next application of mulch.

Reusing household items in the garden

When you garden, it soon becomes apparent what a huge impact you can have on the planet. As well as encouraging biodiversity and supporting wildlife, there may be an opportunity for items you would usually throw away to be reused, recycled or upcycled. Before you put anything in the bin, stop for a moment and think about what you could do with that 'rubbish'. It's great fun to use household items to sow, grow and care for plants.

Toilet roll holders

The cardboard rolls inside the toilet paper are perfect to sow seeds in. Keep them the size they are for sowing seeds that have long roots, such as sweet peas and carrots, or cut them in half, place them on a tray, add your compost and sow to your hearts content.

Plastic food containers

The containers that hold fruit and vegetables are great for seed sowing or using as trays to keep your seed pots on. If you are sowing seeds, make sure there are drainage holes, then add your compost and seeds. Easy, cheap and satisfying.

Washing-up bowls

When your bowl is at the end of its life, make sure there are no holes and use it as a mini wildlife pond. Or, with holes in the base you can use it as a planter, maybe even a fairy garden for you and your children to enjoy!

Plastic bottles

You might need to keep birds away from your fruit and vegetables. If so, an upturned bottle on a bamboo cane can be enough to deter them. Clear plastic bottles are also great if you cut them in half and place over seedlings that need some protection outside.

Nurturing Your Growing Plants

As you start to see your plants leap into growth with more foliage, taller stems and buds appearing, you will begin to feel a great sense of joy and positivity for the future. Think about how your plants started off as tiny seeds in your hand that you've cared for from germination to becoming young plants. Your plants are your responsibility, giving you a reason each day to step outside and be connected to the natural world. Throughout your gardening journey, each step will provide you with new challenges, changes and the ability to continually consider how each moment in the garden relates to your own life as you immerse yourself in the magical pursuit of cultivating plants. You will begin to recognize that support is sometimes needed to ensure plants stay strong, and they will need water and nutrients to nourish from within and flourish on the outside, just like you.

Now your plants are becoming established, you will see just how quickly many will grow. As soon as the sun shines and the soil is warm they will leap into action. New leaf after new leaf will grow, surprisingly fast, buds forming and just waiting to burst into bloom, leaving you in awe of nature's ability to work hard at fulfilling a purpose. During this stage of growth it is important to nourish and nurture those little lives as they mature each day, providing them with the perfect growing conditions to reach their full potential.

Supporting and Protecting

Each of us at times throughout life will need some extra support. When life gets tough, we call on friends and family to help. There is nothing more important than support, guidance and protection when we most need them and they help us move forward with the best people in our lives. Reaching out to others shows strength in recognizing that you are dealing with difficulty and that you need help, and allows you to acknowledge your feelings and emotions so you can start to build more strength towards recovery.

Some of your plants will equally need support as they grow. That may be watering and feeding but also protecting and holding upright as they grow taller. Weather changes can mean wind damage, heavy rain bashing and even the weight of snow burdening plants. Think of each of these as similar to situations that can occur in your life and then you can see how your support for these plants is no different to how we all need help at times as well.

As plants grow tall, use bamboo canes as supports. Gently tie the plants to the bamboo canes with string, which will hold them up, so the stems don't collapse and break. Ideally add the supports before your plants get too big to ensure less root damage. Just like most things in gardening, you can make your own. If you don't have bamboo canes, create supports from wooden stakes, metal pipes, wire mesh and pallets and you can even repurpose old tyres and bike wheels and collect fallen branches for your plants to climb up. There are so many support systems out there just waiting for you to call on them.

Watering Methods

As your plants grow, and especially in dry weather, they will need to be watered to ensure they are hydrated. Watering helps the roots to draw up the nutrients in the soil and transport them up the stem and to the leaves. Without water, you will quickly see plants droop and you will know they need a good soaking to bring them back to life.

Rainwater is by far the best means of watering since that's as nature intended, so try to collect in a water butt or barrel. Then, take a few minutes in the morning to water your plants while you drink your cup of tea, listening to bird song and with your bare feet on the lawn. Starting the day outside in a few moments of mindfulness ticks a lot of wellbeing boxes before you get started on the day ahead.

If mornings are not your thing, early evening is also a great time to enjoy the garden as the light dims and the evening insects go about their business. Maybe you will even spot bats gracefully flitting through the sky during the summer.

The change of dynamic in the garden from morning to evening is exquisite to observe so enjoy either morning or evening or, indeed, any time you get to spend outside.

Your plants will enjoy a thorough watering when needed, which is a better approach than little and often. If you water little and often, the water may only reach a few centimetres into the soil but roots grow far deeper than that, so make sure you're watering deep enough for your plants to thrive. By ensuring the water reaches the roots, you will be helping them to grow bigger and stronger. They will also have more time to absorb the water before it evaporates.

When it comes to what to water with, from hosepipes on reels or expandable hoses that pack away with ease, there are many options. Watering cans are perfect for pots and containers but if you would like to make your own, recycle a large drinks bottle with a plastic lid by punching holes in the lid and then filling the bottle with water. It's a budget-friendly and easy way to water pots and hanging baskets.

Saving Water for the Environment

Saving rainwater is an easy way to keep your garden plants hydrated and it's also beneficial for the environment. As you save each drop of rain, you will know that you are not only limiting tap-water usage but, when the summer is hot and water is in short supply, your plants will still be hydrated with the water nature intended for them. Pots dry out fast so saving water is essential no matter what size garden you have. Rainwater is also great to top up your pond.

Water Butts

Water butts are the easiest way to collect rainwater. You can collect the run-off from your greenhouse or shed by connecting guttering to your water butt, but don't worry if space is limited, as you can also collect rainwater in recycled old barrels and other suitable watertight containers and stand them wherever they fit in the garden. If they are open at the top, cover with a net so that rainwater can get in but wildlife stays out.

Mulch

Mulching your plants (see Feeding Plants for Health, pages 94–5) can drastically reduce water evaporation and even keep the roots cooler during hot spells, meaning your plants won't be so desperate for water. Mulch also improves the soil you are growing in by providing nutrients for your plants. See page 27 for how to make a simple leaf mulch.

Water Wisely

Watering in the morning, especially if you have a lot of slugs and snails, is a good move because they tend to munch on plants at night, plus it helps to prevent fungal diseases that take hold overnight, but evening watering can allow the plants longer to absorb the water they need. Water at the base of the plant so it reaches the roots rather than on the foliage where it will evaporate. You can also reuse your washing up water in the garden on your plants and lawn but avoid using it on edibles. Try not to water during the day to avoid evaporation and wasting your water.

Feeding Plants

Just like us, plants need nutrition to grow. Most will be absorbed from the soil, compost or mulch that you use. However it can be helpful, especially when gardening in pots and containers, to feed your plants when they are in active growth. If you buy plant food, make sure it is organic so you are able to continue creating a beautifully biodiverse garden and always follow the instructions on the label. Making your own feed is of course much more rewarding, enjoyable and cheaper (see Feeding Plants for Health, pages 94–5).

Start in spring by feeding plants once every two weeks and, as your plants grow into their beauty, start to feed them once a week until active growth has finished.

When Things Go Wrong

Some plants will flower quickly and others require more patience and greater nurturing. Either way, all are beautiful in their own right and you can admire the differences in everything you grow. As you continue to nurture your garden, remember that the flowers will bloom soon and each morning when you open your curtains there will be something new to marvel at.

There will also be times of disappointment and times when gardening doesn't quite go as planned. When things go wrong, try not to despair and, although the disappointment at a plant not making it can be upsetting, it's all part of learning and development. When things do go wrong, remember how strong you are, how you can get up, brush it off and move forward. Will your plants survive if they are given extra support and nourishment? Or is it best to simply move on and admire all of the other beauty you've created around you? Making mistakes can be one of the best ways to learn. Don't forget, even the best gardeners in the world don't always get it right. Nature has its own plan sometimes.

As you take joy in the practical side of gardening, make time to simply observe your plants' growth and behaviours. You will notice that plants don't pay much attention to weeds and other challenges around them. They simply look towards the sun, absorbing the rays, as they give little time to obstacles. Of course, sometimes they may need a helping hand from you, to ensure they survive and thrive.

Reach for the sky on your journey and try not to be distracted by influences that can burden you. Just like the life of a plant, there will be ever-changing circumstances and knowing that you can work with that change is a good thing, ensuring you keep your goals and purpose in mind. You may have to step out of your comfort zone sometimes for true growth and even if you aren't sure quite what you are doing, challenges and experimenting can lead to enlightenment and contentment. Plants have evolved and adapted to changes out of their control since time began, but they still carry on growing towards fulfilling their purpose.

Feeding plants for health

Nourishment starts in the soil and ensuring that you know and love your soil is by far the best way of producing wonderful blooms and abundant crops (see Identifying Your Soil Type, page 30). There are other ways we feed plants, especially those growing in pots and containers. Here is a quick guide to keeping your garden well fed:

Feed the soil

Feed your soil with garden compost, leaf mulch (see page 27) and other well-rotted organic matter. This is usually done in spring and autumn. Mulch all of your garden borders, or just around your plants, leaving a little space around the stems. The elements will help the soil absorb the nutrients that the roots will enjoy.

Replenish the soil

The garden can provide everything you need to have balanced and well-fed plants. For a simple natural plant feed, chop up some comfrey or nettle leaves and pack them into a bucket, then top up with water and cover over. In about four weeks it will be ready to dilute and can be used anywhere in the garden. Use about one part feed to ten parts water and dilute it more if the liquid is really dark brown. You don't need to be too precise. Wear gloves when handling the plants and the liquid and be prepared for the smell! Comfrey is particularly good for fruits such as tomatoes and nettle is great for containers full of flowers.

Feed for your pots

Plants growing in pots will soon use up all of the nutrients available in the compost, so to keep them in good shape they will need a feed throughout spring and summer. Using the nettle or comfrey feed is perfect but, alternatively, organic liquid fertilizers can be used at intervals in the growing season to give your plants a boost. These are usually applied mixed with water – always check the label before use.

Watch the feed being absorbed into the soil and imagine the roots taking it in and transporting the goodness through the plant to produce flowers and fruits. We need vitamins and minerals and at times when we feel run down and want to bloom again, good food is top of the list. Your plants need the same.

Weeding, Pruning and Lawn Maintenance

Along the path to contentment, we can progress by accepting, persisting and taking time for self-care. True growth happens when you look after yourself holistically and the same applies in your garden. This chapter encourages you to look at gardening in a new light, from beneficial weeds to pruning with self-growth in mind. Hand in hand with practical gardening advice, there will be reminders to step back and focus or meditate and definitely have some fun.

Learn
to Love
Your Weeds

Weeds are just plants growing where they are unwanted. These plants are generally called 'weeds' because they can be persistent and compete for nutrients with the plants you are cultivating. A plant can be classed as a weed if it is anything that you haven't intentionally grown or it is becoming a problem. There are, of course, also weeds that can inflict damage to land, buildings and other living species. Japanese knotweed is the most well known, but one person's weed can be another person's gold. For example, in the UK agapanthus is regarded as a stunning border and container plant, with its tall stems and burst of firework-style flowers, but in some areas of Australia it can grow out of control and is considered a weed.

When you realize that every single plant is here for a reason, you can start to see that although weeds may not be ideal in your garden, they do serve a purpose. In fact, weeds are an essential part of the ecosystem and having some in your garden can improve the soil, give insects shade and transform uncultivated gardens into wildlife havens.

If you take the approach that everything has a purpose, you can tackle weeding with a whole new frame of mind. Firstly, go easy on yourself if you do have some weeds. There is no need to feel pressured into having a garden that looks perfect, plus you will know that each weed is undoubtedly doing something good, even if you can't see it. However, when cultivating a garden, you will need to allow the plants you want to grow adequate space and nutrients to thrive, which means keeping weeds in check to some extent. You can use this gardening activity to help yourself thrive as well.

Weeding Out the Negative

Weeding not only gives you the opportunity to get stuck into a gardening job that results in immense satisfaction but you can also use it as an opportunity to sort through and discard any negative thoughts you have been experiencing. If you let weeds go to seed, the breeze will help to spread them around your garden so keeping them under control is a good idea. The same applies to negative thoughts: if you let them get bigger they become harder to deal with. Acknowledging your thoughts and emotions and allowing yourself time to sit with them is a good way of starting to deal with them.

Each time you pull out a weed think of a negative thought that you are holding on to. Bring that negative thought to the surface and sit with it for a few moments, viewing it without judgement, simply acknowledging it for what it is – a thought, not a truth.

When you have spent a few moments with those thoughts, start to weed them out. For each negative thought, pull out a weed and think a positive thought in its place.

As you lift each weed, try not to judge it; consider that it has many positive benefits as well. Weeding allows us to re-evaluate negative thoughts within our minds and make space for more positive, wonderful things to grow.

Super weeds

Cleavers (*Galium aparine*), also known as 'sticky willy', is a well-known weed that sticks to clothes and can be great fun (as long as you aren't allergic to it)! It grows large and can smother other plants if left unchecked, but it is actually incredibly useful to cleanse the lymphatic system. It is a diuretic, removing toxins from the body, and is high in vitamin C, along with many other benefits. Pop a handful of the leaves and stems in your smoothie and taste the goodness as your body enjoys the nutrients.

Dandelion (*Taraxacum officinale*) is another well-known plant, commonly considered a weed. However, it is an essential early source of nectar for bees and has a whole host of wellbeing benefits for us. Dandelion fights inflammation in the body, can boost our immune system and is used in anti-ageing skin care. Dandelion tea is easy to make: just steep the flowers or foliage and add a little

ʿWays to Weed

There are many ways to weed, each with benefits, and weeding can be an individual or group task where you can pass time being connected to your soil and plants.

A **garden hoe** is your friend. It is one of the easiest ways to remove small, annual weeds before they get too big and take over. Hoeing provides some light physical activity

something sweet, if desired. The roots are the most valuable in terms of medicinal properties but the whole plant is edible and, in addition to tea, can be used to make coffee and even wine.

Stinging nettles (*Urtica dioica*) are not only great for making plant feed but they are home to ladybirds, loved by red admiral butterflies and many other beneficial insects in the garden. Nettles are packed full of vitamins A, C, K, B and many minerals. Nettle tea is an easy and quick way to enjoy all of the benefits – simply steep a handful of leaves and add a dash of lemon juice, if desired.

as you sweep the weeds away just below the surface of the soil. Doing this on a dry day makes it much easier to remove the dead weeds from the soil.

Hand forks are particularly useful if you have raised beds or containers, or if you would like to weed on your hands and knees. You can gently loosen the soil and remove the weeds by hand. Taking your time to pull each weed and watch as the soil becomes clear is a good way to make sure you have pulled all of them.

A **fork** or **spade** might be needed to remove large weeds. Particularly difficult to remove perennial weeds, such as docks and couch grass, will need to be dug out. Enjoy the process and exertion of dealing with these types of weeds, as they can be the most gratifying to finally remove.

There will likely be a particular weed that loves your garden, but this can give you an indication of what soil type you have. If you have nettles for example, your soil is likely to be full of nitrogen, which is an important nutrient for plants. It may be better to work with some weeds than against them, just keeping some under control by cutting back or pruning as and when needed. Accept that all plants have a purpose and you will come across many weeds as you garden. When you pull each weed, see if you can identify it and are able to use it in your food, drinks or cosmetics for health benefits.

Pruning Out the Old

During our progression through life we sometimes have to remind ourselves that our past does not determine our future. It can be hard to let go of the past, but by working on the changes you need to make in your own life alongside working in your garden, you will start to build confidence to move on from feelings, people and situations that are holding you back.

You will find, as you prune, that removing unwanted plant material is a lot like taking control and moving on from negative thoughts from the past. By pruning your plants, you can see how to reframe your future and, as you compost your garden waste, any negativity from previous experiences can be disposed of in that same pile of composted plants.

Pruning, Trimming and Deadheading

All of these may be referred to as pruning, but there are slight variations to each. *Pruning* is generally used to stimulate growth by removing branches and stems, to eliminate diseases and to create shape and good air flow. *Trimming* is more to do with tidying up, cutting out

Herbal heaven

Herbs are the some of the most beneficial plants we can grow and have been used medicinally and in cosmetics since before records began. Growing herbs to help with your own health and wellbeing is an empowering process. Try some of these easy herbal fixes during your day:

- Rose and chamomile blend perfectly in a cup of tea. Chamomile is calming and rose can improve digestion. Together the flavour is delicately sweet and fragrantly relaxing.

- For an invigorating pick-me-up pop mint, lemon balm and lime into a jug of water and feel your whole spirit get a boost of healthy goodness.

- Iced tea can be a refreshing treat, especially in the summer as you take a break from gardening. Fennel and nettle work well together to boost your immune system and may even help your memory.

- Add lavender to gin and tonic, mint to a mojito and basil to your strawberry daiquiri. And freeze sprigs of a favourite herb along with the water in your ice-cube tray to add to all kinds of drinks.

- Most herbs can be brewed fresh in teas but don't forget to dry some for using over the winter months. They can also be washed and then frozen in bags.

overgrown parts of the plant and making the plant look good. **Deadheading** is removing faded flowers before they set seed which is a helpful boost to encourage more flowers to grow.

Tools of the Trade

To prune effectively your tools need to be clean and sharp. If you use blunt tools, the cut you make can stress the plant which may become diseased. If you invest in a good set of secateurs, they can last a lifetime and be your go-to for many gardening jobs, including harvesting. Garden scissors are useful for delicate work and cutting soft stems. Loppers are used for cutting thicker stems and branches and you can even use long pruners for those harder to reach branches. Garden saws can be used as well for the bigger jobs.

There are prickly, sharp or toxic plants that you will need to wear gloves for when pruning. Heavy-duty gloves will save your hands when pruning anything unsafe but lighter-weight gloves are great for most pruning if the plants are safe.

If you are pruning or trimming small amounts, simply use a bucket to collect waste material before transferring to the compost pile. If you are pruning on a large scale, such as an ivy hedge, lay old bed sheets on the ground

Some common plants to prune, trim and deadhead

Box hedging (*Buxus sempervirens*) can be trimmed from mid- to late summer; don't leave it too late as it needs time to recover before winter. You can snip it into so many shapes, by trimming in spring and then again in summer, creating your very own piece of topiary artwork.

Lavender (*Lavandula*) can be trimmed lightly in spring and then cut back after flowering. In order to ensure your plant will produce flowers again the following year, don't prune into the old woody stems. Don't forget to save removed flowers, which can be hung upside down with string to dry out (see Easy Storage Hacks, page 143) and then you can use them in cosmetics, baking and to make scented pillows to aid sleep.

Rose (*Rosa*) pruning depends very much on the type of rose you are growing so always check first but generally remove diseased, dead and any stems that cross over, in late winter to early spring. This will help to allow light and good air flow through the centre of your rose.

Raspberry (*Rubus idaeus*) pruning is based on what time of year they fruit. If your raspberries fruit in the summer, cut back after fruiting down to the ground, leaving the strongest young canes for the following year. Autumn-fruiting raspberries will fruit the following year from the current season's growth, so you can cut all of the canes to the ground in early spring.

Dogwood (*Cornus*) has the most fiery-coloured stems and to be able to enjoy them for as long as possible, after the first couple of years, hard prune them in early spring down to the ground or remove dead, damaged and crossing stems first then prune back the remaining stems but not quite as hard, leaving the height of two nodes on the stems, which are easy to see. You can prune them from late winter but equally leave them until mid springtime, when there is also some new growth.

Zinnia, dahlia, cosmos, petunias and marigolds (*Tagetes*), along with many more flowers, all benefit from deadheading. Snip the stem just below the base of the flower after it has faded. This means the plant will focus energy into growing more flowers, since the purpose is to set seed and produce more plants! Of course, if you are seed-saving then leave some flowers to collect the seeds later (see page 110).

that the pruned material can fall onto and that can then be scooped up to dispose of – it can save a lot of time sweeping up afterwards.

What Do You Need to Prune?

Pruning depends on the plants you are growing, their rate of growth and health. These factors have to be considered when deciding what, when and how to prune. It's good practice to have a notebook of all of the plants, shrubs and trees you have in the garden so you can keep a record of what you have growing and refer to it when needed. It is also well worth doing some research before pruning to make sure you are doing it at the right time of year for the plant and jotting this down in your notebook for following years.

There are numerous techniques for and times to prune, so know your plants and take time to research and really get to know their needs. When you prune and watch your plants grow, you will see how they don't hang on to the old or miss what's gone, they simply strive to flourish in the future.

As you snip or saw off each stem or branch, think about something you feel is holding you back. Each time you make the cut, view this as cutting ties with negative aspects of your past and allow them to fall away, making room for healthy new growth. Over the seasons watch how the plants you have pruned grow stronger and bloom again, with even more beauty. Then you will see how removing unwanted past experiences and going easier on yourself can mean that you, too, will flourish.

Sustainable Gardening for the Bigger Picture

It is easy to think that what we do in our day-to-day lives doesn't matter to the wider world, but every step you take and every decision you make have an impact. And there is no better place than the garden to ensure your impact is a positive one.

Sustainable gardening is approaching how you garden in an environmentally friendly way, giving back to and enhancing the natural world by using green methods of gardening. This includes looking after your soil, reducing waste, conserving water, composting and nourishing yourself and your family with plants for happiness in all ways, from aesthetics to nutrition.

Gardening sustainably is a lifestyle choice; it teaches us to look closely at everything we do and to accept that we are a small part of a much bigger picture, along with all other species, in the planetary ecosystem. When you garden sustainably you will be making things better than when you started, not just for yourself but for everything around you and all that we share this planet with.

Ways to Garden Sustainably

Seed-saving is not only a mindful activity, as you focus on collecting the seedheads and carefully putting the seeds into packets, but it's also a way to continue the cycle of growth, save money, grow your favourite plants year after year, protect biodiversity and truly understand the life cycle of your plants.

Saving seeds means you don't have to rely on purchasing them and the plants you grow will have become well adapted to growing in your garden. It is incredibly easy to do: on a dry day after flowering, when the seeds have set, collect the seeds and store them in a paper bag in a cool, dry place. Don't forget to label them with the name, collecting date and any notes.

Growing the right plants is essential when it comes to gardening sustainably. By choosing mostly native plants, you may reduce pests and diseases. Native plants will be more adapted to your growing conditions and many are loved by wildlife that will feed on pests, they also ensure food sources and homes for wildlife are available. Native plants can also make gardening much easier as they are naturally suited to the climate. Wildflowers are a lovely way to brighten up a bare patch and invite pollinators in.

Organic gardening is the most positive way to look after your garden and the wider environment. There are many organic ways to control weeds, pests and diseases, some of which have already been mentioned (see Companion Planting, pages 72–5). Widespread use of chemical treatments has already contributed to a huge decline in insects but by using organic methods you can welcome all little creatures and protect biodiversity. Avoid pesticides and herbicides to give your garden the best chance of thriving.

Veganic gardening includes all that organic gardening does, but it also means that no animal products, such as manure or blood, fish and bone fertilizers, are used. It ensures harm to animals is minimized in the process of cultivating plants.

Material Usage

Reuse and recycle is the way forward, and that includes materials from the garden. If you have redesigned your garden and taken out some old fence panels, think of ways that you can reuse the wood. The same applies for paving stones or bricks that can be reused to make a fire pit or pot feet, for example. They can all be used for creative ideas to both save money and reduce landfill. When buying new items for the garden, look for sustainably resourced products and even consider what you will do with it when it is past its best.

ZERO WASTE

A zero-waste garden, in which everything is reused in the garden to help nature thrive, can provide wonderful peace of mind. As you rest at night you can satisfy yourself that you are contributing positively to the environment. Zero waste means no plastic, or at least recycling all plastic items as much as you can, and making sure your garden purchases are considered before buying, such as good-quality tools and equipment that will last. Repairing items instead of throwing away is another way to reduce waste, and don't forget the compost heap! It's a great place to allow materials to rot down and give back to your soil.

PEAT-FREE COMPOST

When you buy compost, you will see that most includes peat. Peat is a natural resource from peat bogs that provide important habitats for species that live there. Gardening with peat-free compost ensures that you are protecting peat bogs and all that thrive in them. You will also be lessening the carbon omissions they release when harvested which contributes to climate change. Peat-free compost will be labelled as such on the bag, so you can easily find it.

At times it can be overwhelming when we think about the changes needed to protect the environment, but when you focus on gardening sustainably you will discover an illuminating opportunity to work closely with mother nature and when it's just you and your plants, it really can be as simple as just looking out for each other.

Mowing
Your Lawn

One of the great joys of gardening is the satisfaction felt when you have just mowed the lawn. When the lawn gets a haircut, it's as though the whole garden has had a tidy up. From the aroma of freshly mowed grass clippings to the sharp edges trimmed to perfection, the look and feel of a well-kept lawn is one of the many wonderful aspects of a garden.

There is much more to your lawn than meets the eye. Lawns are home to many beneficial insects, such as beetles and worms, and to so many invertebrates that you will often see your garden birds pottering around enjoying a feed. Lawns also help with natural rainwater drainage, soil erosion (as the roots bind the soil) and even clean the air by absorbing pollutants and taking in carbon dioxide to release oxygen.

Mowing the lawn is not only a great way to burn some calories with a burst of satisfying physical exercise but the repetitive action of pushing a mower really is quite calming for the mind. Focusing on mowing allows you time to concentrate on achieving something fairly quickly, when a lot of other gardening tasks can require much more patience. While mowing the lawn is quite a simple task, you may at times find you encounter obstacles such as trees, pathways or even mole hills and wet patches that you need to work around. This small-scale example of thinking about and overcoming obstacles is a great skill to learn for larger challenges that life may throw our way. When obstacles arise in our lives, overcoming them can make us feel wonderfully triumphant.

A Healthy Lawn

Keeping your lawn in good shape will ensure it stays healthy, neat and even. Mowing takes place from spring to autumn at weekly intervals and sometimes, if you want a short, formal cut you will get a workout twice a week!

When you first dust down the mower in spring, give it a clean, make sure the blades are sharp and check it over before you get going, then cut on the highest setting so you don't shock the lawn with a close shave. Each time you mow, gradually lower the setting until you are mowing at the height you want to keep the grass. If you cut too close, you will find it will need watering more and there could be bare patches, moss and unwanted weeds. Don't waste the grass clippings – you can compost them, use them in your no-dig bed (see page 83) or even leave some on your lawn to provide a natural fertilizer.

When to water your lawn is really up to you but the less you water, the better for the environment. Generally when the lawn begins to fade, give it a water in the morning or evening to avoid evaporation when it is warm during the day. It is better to give it a deep water infrequently than water little and often. But bear in mind grass is incredibly resilient. Even if it dries out, it will regrow when the conditions improve.

If your lawn needs a little lift, during spring when the temperature warms up but the soil hasn't dried out, try scarifying to remove weeds and moss. Use a scarifier which will loosen the soil and rake away the debris. If you are left with bare patches, top dress (sprinkle fine compost) onto the bare areas and sow some lawn seed. Keep it moist and you will see new shoots in no time.

Aerating your lawn is another way to keep it in good shape. If you have a lawn that is particularly well used and becoming hard and dry use a garden fork or a special aeration tool to make holes in the lawn during spring. It helps the soil to absorb water, nutrients and air which can lead to improved grass health.

Alternative Lawns

Your lawn doesn't have to be perfect green grass. In fact, chamomile (*Chamaemelum nobile*) and creeping thyme (*Thymus serpyllum*) lawns were once very common, documented long before the formal lawn become popular. Both can cover ground quickly and still thrive if only walked on occasionally.

Creeping thyme will not only provide a green space in your garden but also produces pretty pink flowers during the summer and is simply divine to see. It has a lovely scent too as you crush or walk on it. You can use it for creating teas, tinctures and in cooking, plus honey bees and other pollinators like to indulge in the nectar. Creeping thyme will need far less water than a grass lawn to maintain, plus if mowing isn't your thing, a cut back twice a year is enough. The easiest way to establish a flowering lawn is to purchase plug plants (mini plants) and plant out about 15cm (6in) apart in a pre-weeded, sunny spot. They work well in smaller areas and if you don't want to walk on it, put down some stepping stones for a most pleasing path that the thyme will grow around.

Chamomile is also an option for an alternative to a grass lawn, and not only provides a lovely green space in the garden but a whole host of medicinal benefits too. Chamomile is a calming herb, easing anxiety, settling stomach issues and much more. As with creeping thyme, starting with plug plants can help the lawn to establish quicker or you can sow seeds under cover, transplant to pots and then plant out when they are a little bigger, during late spring. Chamomile needs sun or very light shade and will only need a trim once a year, or after flowering. You can walk lightly on a chamomile lawn if you want to, but not until it is well established. It will be worth the wait!

No Mow

If you decide to allow your lawn to go wild, you might be surprised at what will grow. Imagine spotting wild orchids, oxeye daisies and cowslips growing just outside your window. It's extraordinary to see what happens when nature is allowed breathing space. If you don't want your whole lawn to go wild, experiment by allocating a space that you mow around so you can watch what grows in this special wild patch.

The no-mow approach benefits the environment by supporting biodiversity and providing habitats for wildlife as the wildflowers already hiding in your lawn will be given the opportunity to bloom and the taller grass will provide shelter for insects.

There are numerous approaches, from only starting to mow at the end of mid-summer to enjoy the spring and early summer wildflowers, or not mowing for a couple of months from late spring to early summer, or instead of mowing weekly, let your grass grow longer and mow every three or so weeks.

Mix It Up

One of the many advantages of having a lawn is that it provides you with the opportunity to experiment and mix things up! As your confidence grows in the garden, you will discover a yearning to experiment and discover just how much you can be surprised by nature. You could sow your own choice of wildflowers in the lawn, with loose seeds or seed balls, directly where you would like them to grow. Why not combine all of the suggestions and keep your lawn, a pathway with creeping thyme growing around (see illustration below), a pot full of chamomile and an area for wildflowers? You don't even need a big space to shake things up, let your imagination run wild and be filled with fascination for what will grow.

Whichever way you choose to grow and maintain your lawn, feel pride in taking care of something so important to wildlife and remember to walk on it, play on it and admire it in whatever form it takes. Even something that is perceived to be simple, like a lawn, can fill you with fascination and joy.

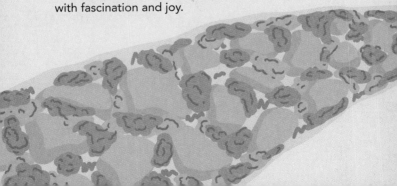

Making the Most of Your Lawn

The interconnectedness of physical activity and mental wellbeing has been well-documented – even just short bursts can lift our mood and help to reduce stress and anxiety.[6] Gardening is a great way to get exercise, from the gentle movements made while watering seedlings to the more intense body workout when digging the soil. As you garden your physical wellbeing is being looked after.

EXERCISING IN THE GARDEN

There are other ways of incorporating exercise into your daily routine when you are in your garden. The space you have created can be used in many ways and to exercise, whatever that looks like to you, is one of them.

Stretching and yoga

Take a moment to stand outside and stretch your arms high into the air, feel the stretch from your core all the way to the tips of your fingers. Breathe in deeply through your nose and out through your mouth. Bring your hands back down to your chest, palms together, and repeat five times. You should feel relaxed and aware of the sounds and smells around you. Move on to stretching your whole body or do some yoga surrounded by your plants.

Circuit training

If you want to go all out, but don't have time to go to an exercise class, the garden is an ideal place to work out. Make your own circuit training with items from your shed, such as mini high jumps made from plant tunnels, lift pots or homegrown vegetables as weights, and lay bags of compost or pots on the lawn to run around and jump over. Afterwards, don't forget to stretch, place your hands on the lawn and feel your connection to the planet.

FUN AND GAMES

Your garden can be a place of peace, time out and respite but it can also be transformed into a hive of entertainment and laughter by inviting friends and family over to share your special place. Sociability is an essential part of wellbeing and where better to feel close to those you love than in your own garden? From barbecues to evening drinks, picnics to hide and seek, have some fun.

Giant lawn games

From Jenga to chess, oversized lawn games are an entertaining way to spend time outside with friends. Children will especially love running around barefoot on the lawn, working out puzzles and laughing as the Jenga tower tumbles over.

Cornhole competition

If you'd prefer something calmer, highly addictive cornhole is a competitive game friends can play together for hours. Traditionally, a small bag of corn kernels is thrown through a hole on a raised wooden platform. You can make your own bean bags instead and have fun taking turns to see who is the first to get it in the hole.

Treasure hunt

Send the kids off on a hunt around the garden for nature-inspired treasure. Look for different colour flowers, find a bug, a pebble, a specific leaf. Both fun and educational!

Whatever games you plan, talk to your friends about your journey in the garden, your favourite plants, the wildlife you enjoy spotting. Be proud of your achievements and share your love of the garden.

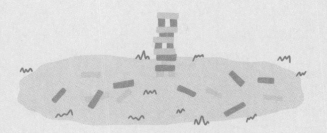

Understanding Pests

Tiny creatures in the garden are generally considered to be either friend or foe to the gardener. Will they eat your plants or will they eat the pests that eat your plants? Challenge yourself to rethink your perception of garden pests and try to view all pests as friends. It's definitely difficult to do when something is munching on your new shoots, but by accepting that each and every one is contributing to the ecosystem and indeed the wider environment, you can start to see pests in a more holistic way.

When you spot unwanted insects on your plants, you might feel panic, disappointment or frustration but give yourself a moment to slow down, watch them in detail and even try to embrace their presence. We find ourselves with these same emotions at many points in our lives but allow yourself the time to work out what the best approach is before making a decision too soon. Persistence and patience pay off if you are faced with a daunting situation.

All garden insects are performing a function and have their purpose, even though you would prefer their purpose not to be ruining your flower or vegetable beds! When you stop for a moment you can take time to observe their behaviour and check the plants nearby to see if they are spreading. If you have made a thriving environment for wildlife, you may also soon spot a predator moving in to sort out the issue for you. If you find aphids, you will also see the ladybird army coming in to feast on them. For infestations like this, it truly can be beneficial to let nature take its course.

Managing pests is often the better answer than trying to eradicate them. This is when a flourishing ecosystem really comes into its own. Hedgehogs will eat earwigs and slugs. Bats eat gnats and mosquitoes. Frogs and toads eat spiders and slugs. Birds eat many insects and some will even eat mice. Lacewings eat aphids and mites. If you know what pests your plants are prone to, you can then plant specifically to attract the predators that will control the problem for you.

If you find garden pests that are out of control and persistent, there are many organic ways to stop them spreading further and prevent diseases and damage. Prevention is always better than cure.

Good Plant Health

Keeping your pots and tools clean to prevent pests is one way to ensure they don't spread. Clean garden structures like coldframes, greenhouses, polytunnels to make sure pests such as red spider mite can't shelter there over winter. Look after your plants, keeping them healthy, planting out at the right time of year and protecting them as needed. Stressed plants can be a magnet for pests.

Sacrificial Crops

Planting specifically to deter pests away from one plant towards another is a really good natural way to protect the plants you want to bloom or harvest. Nasturtiums (*Tropaeolum majus*) are a feast for cabbage white butterflies which will keep them off your brassicas. Plant lettuce around your garden beds for the snails to munch, giving them something other than your dahlia and hosta shoots to enjoy (see Companion Planting, pages 72–5).

Crop Rotation

Pests and diseases can build up in the soil, so crop rotation is important, especially if you are growing edibles. Try not to plant the same crop in the same place every year and work on a four-year crop rotation plan where your

potatoes in year one are followed by legumes
(runner beans/climbing beans/peas) in year two;
year three would be brassicas (cabbages/kale/
broccoli) and in year four plant onions and root
vegetables (turnips/carrots).

Safe Netting

For good plant protection from birds and
butterflies, always have some fine netting at hand. It can
be used over cages, frames and DIY pipe tunnels (flexible
pipes made into hoops to lay netting over) as a wildlife-
friendly deterrent. However, do make sure the netting is
securely fixed to the ground with pegs, wood or heavy
rocks so birds and other wildlife can't get inside and
become trapped.

DIY Protection

Especially if you have lots of pigeons around, it can be
helpful to keep them away from your young plants. Try
spacing a few upturned bottles on bamboo canes around
your plants so that the noise and movements of the
bottles in the wind help to steer these birds away from
your plants. You could also tie old CDs on string and hang
them around, which will distract birds.

Plant Collars

These slip around the base of the young stem and protect
plants, mainly in the brassica family, from root fly which can
destroy plants. Some also include copper which slugs and
snails may avoid so they are a double prevention!

Letting Nature Find Its Own Way

Accepting that sometimes you might lose a plant or even a full crop of vegetables and knowing that even though it can be heartbreaking, you have given a home and supplied food to another species that you share this planet with, can lift the sadness of losing a precious plant. What you are aiming for is to protect your plants, not to eradicate pests.

As you continue to nurture your garden, be captivated by all the creatures that visit. Tiny ants don't cause much damage to the garden but they work incredibly hard, just like they are trying to save the world – and that's because they actually are.[7] We need those tiny little creatures busily working away around our feet. Watch them and you may find yourself enchanted.

Pay close attention to the circle of life in the garden, how all wildlife rely on each other and are also impacted by your actions. It can help us to accept that sometimes, as in life, it can be best just to let it be.

Taking a Meditative Time-Out

Many times, you will be busy in the garden enjoying some physical exercise, other moments you will be deep in thought about the task at hand, but sometimes it's good practice to simply think of nothing at all.

Our thoughts determine how we feel so by taking time to recognize our thought patterns and make them more positive, we can improve our overall wellbeing. Our minds often become consumed with everyday stresses combined with experiences from the past and worries for the future, and the way we deal with our thoughts can become muddled, often resulting in anxiety and depression.

This is a simple way to calm a busy brain into a meditative state of not really thinking about much at all:

1. Find a place in your garden and take a seat. This can be on the ground or a chair, wherever is most comfortable for you.
2. Think of a statement that you can use when thoughts arise as you relax into clearing your mind – perhaps 'I am strong' or 'I believe'.
3. Close your eyes and breathe in through your nose for five seconds and then out through your mouth for ten seconds. Do this a few times until you feel completely relaxed.
4. Practise clearing your mind of all worries and thinking of nothing.

5. When a thought comes to mind, say your statement to distract you from your thoughts. You can do this out loud or in your head.

6. Repeat as much as needed for about 10 minutes and build up to 20 minutes over time if that feels comfortable. It is your practice, so you will know when you are finished.

7. When you open your eyes, allow yourself a couple of minutes to adjust before you get up.

When practising this kind of meditation, thoughts can drift in but let them go and just be in the moment. If you don't want to close your eyes, just stare into the grass, up at the sky or at a specific plant but, instead of looking at the detail, focus on nothing at all. Sit still, breathe, relax. These moments are precious.

Immersing Yourself in Bug Life and Bird Song

By creating a biodiverse garden and observing the changes as it evolves, you will notice wildlife enjoying your space with you. Catching a glimpse of your favourite garden bird or a nest and hatchlings can be a moment of pure marvel, as you appreciate how important your space is to wildlife as well as you. The benefits of this two-way relationship are immense and when you take notice of how everything is connected around you, you can acknowledge what your impact has been on the many creatures that are enjoying life in among your plants.

Fascinating Bug Life

Often children are enthralled by bugs, turning a stone to see the life beneath – beetles, woodlice, centipedes, each busy going about their day. But as we grow, that fascination can wane even though those bugs are still there under those stones, pots and garden ornaments, going about their business, helping your garden to thrive.

Try recapturing that childish curiosity: turn over a rock or a piece of wood in your garden and see what you can find. There might be worm holes, perhaps a snail or two, you may even find a gloriously interesting stag beetle. Studying each insect can build a true sense of wonder that each one is contributing to your garden space and they will carry on with their lives after you gently replace their shelter.

Morning Bird Song

When you hear the birds singing, stop for a moment and indulge yourself in nature's enchanting music. Our feathered friends bring a wonderful dynamic to the garden, as they nest, fledge, feed and sleep. Bird song will increase in a thriving garden as birds begin to establish their own territory and if you step outside with the intention of listening to the music, you will feel a warm satisfaction knowing that you have helped to provide homes and food that birds can enjoy.

The dawn chorus is one of the most incredible ways to awaken the mind in the morning; the sound is one of reassurance that the day has begun. Bird song can bring a feeling of safety and security, and as such it is a wonderful antidote to stress. Try standing barefoot on the lawn on a mild morning, close your eyes and allow yourself to start the day immersed in the natural world.

The Evening Reset

A garden abundant with wildlife comes alive with sounds in the evening too: the fluttering of moths, perhaps a bat gliding through the sky. Maybe you will hear grasshoppers or crickets, toads and frogs croaking and the rustle of a hedgehog shuffling along, enjoying an evening excursion. If you have a larger garden, you may even be visited by a fox or an owl. It's exciting to know how much life is active after the sun goes down and the moon is shining in the sky. If you are focused enough to clear your mind, the tiny patter of many insect feet can be heard. It will feel like a whole new world has awakened in your own garden. We usually hide away at night, but if you can take a moment to step outside, this connection with a hive of night-time activity can be just the reset needed to clear the mind in preparation for a good night's rest.

Take the time to listen to, watch and learn about your garden visitors. You will start to feel a responsibility for them and get to know their behaviours and the plants they love. You will achieve an even greater appreciation and understanding of the importance of being connected to everything in your garden.

Harvesting
for Health

Whether you are cutting flowers for the vase
or picking tomatoes for your salad,
harvesting is the time that you can truly
appreciate what happens when you cherish
and nurture plants in your outdoor space.
As you read about the joy of harvesting
throughout this chapter, from health matters
to cooking, sharing your experience then
starting all over again, remember to give
gratitude for your crops at this point of
abundance. Try to keep hold of the joyful
moments when you are reaping the rewards
of your growing and celebrate your
gardening achievements.

Harvest Time

Healthy harvests come from good soil, sustainable and organic gardening practices and the love and care you give your plants. Throughout the gardening process you have been nurturing your own physical and mental health wellbeing as well as the food and flowers you harvest. In busy times, our health often slips down the priority list until we are forced to pay attention to it. When we practise mindful gardening, we are encouraged to continually check in with our physical and mental wellbeing, meaning we are able to recognize changes and take action quickly…much as we do when we nurture our plants.

Harvesting is the moment of celebration: as you pick your flowers or lift your root vegetables, you can enjoy how your hard work has paid off. You will see that some plants needed extra care to get to this point and others have successfully grown without much attention. The same applies to aspects of your physical and mental health wellbeing, and the parts that need more or less attention will be individual to each person. As with our plants, it is through close attention to our own wellbeing that we can discover our pressure points, triggers and unique needs.

Harvesting Methods

You will find that there are different harvesting methods depending on your crop. Here are some examples:

Cut flowers are a lovely addition to the house, but you might find they have some bugs hiding in the petals. After cutting the stems, turn the flowers upside down over a piece of white paper for a short time and you will see most bugs drop off. Set the paper down on the ground outside for 20 minutes or so, until the bugs have escaped back into the garden. Snip off the lower foliage on the stems so it doesn't rot in the water and pop the flowers into a vase. If you aren't arranging them straightaway, dampen some tissue and wrap it around the base of the stems to keep them moist and keep the flowers away from direct sunlight so they don't wilt.

Root vegetables mostly do their growing hidden away under the soil, from turnips, beetroot and carrots to parsnips, radish and Jerusalem artichoke. If you have loose soil you might be able to simply lift some of the smaller vegetables by hand and wipe away the soil. For the larger or deeper-rooted vegetables, such as parsnips, you may need to use a garden fork to loosen the soil before lifting. Gently fork around the root, taking care not to fork into the vegetables, then simply lift them. You may well find that your root veggies have grown in all kinds of wonky ways – they will be no less tasty and are still perfectly good to eat, so embrace the quirks!

Potatoes are easy to harvest, if you have grown them in a bag – simply tip it up and get hunting for potatoes in the compost. If they are in the ground, you will need a fork to dig in and lift the potatoes out. Generally, container-grown potatoes are smaller than those grown in the ground but no less delicious. Have a good search in the soil as they are often hiding deep down and around the plant.

Brassicas will all be harvested slightly differently. Brussels sprouts, for example, are best after the first frost and usually harvested from the bottom of the stalk upwards or you can cut off the whole stalk. Cabbages and cauliflower can be dug up entirely or cut at the stem for a quick harvest and the roots removed later. Sprouting broccoli stems can be snipped when the florets have developed but before they flower – by harvesting at this time, more will then grow. Kale leaves can be harvested from the bottom upwards, ideally before they get too big because the younger leaves taste better.

Legumes including peas, runner beans, broad beans, French bean and soya beans are rich in protein and can be harvested with just a snip above the pod. Some, such as broad beans, will then need to be taken out of their pods and others, like runner beans, can be cooked or frozen as they are harvested.

Salad leaves can be harvested for many months of the year, if you have grown cut-and-come-again leaves. You simply cut the leaves and let more grow until the plant is tired out, at which point you remove the plant and then pick leaves from later-sown salad crops. This is called successional sowing where you sow a particular vegetable about two weeks apart throughout the growing season. You can harvest spinach, chard, mustard and lettuce in this way. If you have grown a full lettuce head, harvest it by pulling the whole plant up and cutting off the stem and roots for the compost pile. Alternatively, you can take the older leaves around the outside of the lettuce first, allowing more space for the lettuce to continue growing. Another option is to cut the lettuce above the base, leaving just a few centimetres of the leaves, which will allow more lettuce to grow during the same season.

Greenhouse crops that are typically grown under cover, such as cucumber, tomatoes, aubergine and chilies, can all be harvested by cutting the stem just above the matured fruit. Tomatoes often can simply be pulled gently from the plant or harvested as a whole vine, depending on the variety you have grown. Try eating them as soon as they are picked as a snack as you garden.

When you harvest your crops, think about how this is also part of making healthy eating choices for yourself and your family. The fresh fruit and vegetables grown with your own hands will make eating nutritious, organic food much easier, plus the flavour is almost always more juicy, sweeter and more fulfilling than supermarket-bought fruit and vegetables. There may even be vegetables that you have never liked but relish when you grow your own.

Harvesting with Gratitude

Embrace the empowering moments as you lift potatoes from the soil, feel the earth slip away from your carrots and the abundance of green goodness as you snip off lettuce, spinach and chard leaves. Smell the fresh tomato harvest and feel the crinkly kale foliage between your fingers. Twirl your cut sunflowers so you can embrace every detail in something you have helped to create. Lay your cosmos, chrysanthemums and calendula out in front of you so you can appreciate the stems, petals and different colours. Don't miss a detail because this is what you have been working towards.

You have shown strength, a willingness to learn and resilience in creating this abundant crop of flowers, fruits and vegetables. And on top of that you have helped provide shelter and sustenance for native wildlife and encouraged the wider ecosystem. That's no mean feat.

Celebrate your hard work with gratitude and try this exercise:

1. With a harvest in front on you, take a seat and close your eyes.
2. Breathe deeply in through your nose and out through your mouth. Repeat until you are feeling calm and relaxed.
3. If other thoughts pop up in your mind, return your focus to the harvest in front of you.
4. Bring your attention to your heart, feel it fill with love and gratitude for yourself and what you have grown. Feel grateful for the abundance of nutritious food in your harvest that will nourish your body and your soul.

5. When you are ready, say the following gratitude affirmations either out loud or in your mind:

'I am grateful for the abundance of crops that nourish my body and soul.'

'I am so happy and grateful to have nutritious food that I have grown.'

'I see the beauty in nature, plants and the environment.'

'I am grateful for my healthy body and mind.'

'I am thankful for what nature provides me.'

'I am truly blessed.'

6. Feel your heart grow with gratitude. Smile, lift your chest high, open up your heart and feel happiness. Say the affirmations as many times as you want to.

7. When you are ready, open your eyes and look at your crops. Recognize that you've grown them on a fulfilling journey of discovery.

Easy storage hacks

When you grow your own food, it's exciting to research recipes ready to get cooking. But sometimes you might have more fruit, vegetables and herbs than you have room for or can cook quick enough. When you have frozen all you can and cooked some to eat fresh, where do you store the rest? It's time to get creative with space and items around the house. Try these simple ideas:

Using tights and stockings

Don't throw out your tights if they get holes. Keep them safe in the corner of your drawer to use when the onion and garlic harvest is ready. Push an onion or garlic bulb in all the way to the foot on one leg and then tie a knot just above the top of the onion or garlic, then put another in and tie another knot. You can do this all the way to the top of the tights and then hang them up on a hook or door handle. It's a great space saver.

Always have string to hand

String is a most helpful accessory to have when you garden and one easy way to dry lavender and other herbs, such as rosemary, thyme and sage, is to make them into bunting. Hang a piece of string in a cool, dry space securing each end on a hook to the wall or ceiling – use a piece of string long enough to hold all of your bunched herbs. Tie each herb in bunches and then attach these to the string using the tie on the bunches. This natural bunting is quick to make and will smell incredible.

Smoothie bags

Freeze your freshly harvested fruit and vegetables in freezer bags to make smoothies on the run. To each bag add a mix of raspberries, blackberries, spinach, chopped cucumber and celery – whatever you have and whatever you enjoy, to create a bag of goodness. When you want to make your smoothie, it will all be there ready for you to add straight to the blender.

Cooking for Comfort

With your abundance of crops at the ready, it's time to get cooking! Growing your own food can help to encourage all of the family to eat a nutritious diet for better overall health. Not only that, but you can even improve your culinary skills by experimenting with new recipes, herbs and spices. Even if you sometimes feel that cooking is a chore, when you use freshly picked produce you will discover an eagerness to see what you can make with it all.

Eating delicious meals full of plants from your garden is the ultimate goal of a vegetable gardener. When you reach this point, enjoy the excitement of tantalizing your taste buds and nourishing your body with fruit and vegetables grown by you, in your soil, during your gardening journey. It will be like placing the last piece of a jigsaw in the picture as everything links together and every bit of your gardening work comes to fruition.

It's a win-win situation! You'll be saving money, decreasing packaging, limiting food miles and you'll know exactly what you are eating and how it was grown. And, along with the financial and nutritional benefits of cooking fresh plant-based food, there are numerous reasons why it is also a positive activity for both your mental and physical wellbeing.

Time for Self-care

The act of cooking is a wonderful way to express creativity and a focused task that can provide a valuable moment of mindfulness. If you feel anxious or stressed, focusing on cooking can help stop negative thoughts in their tracks as you concentrate on reading instructions, weighing ingredients, stirring, checking temperatures and watching it all coming together. You may be following an online cooking forum suggestion, using an old family recipe or making a brand-new dish – whatever you are cooking you should feel empowered as you take on such a mindful task.

You will know what vegetables you will be harvesting so you can plan meals in advance and research recipes you'd like to try. Organize a recipe book where you can collect cut-outs from magazines and newspapers or write out your own ideas. Planning your meals is another focused task that can give your mind a break from stressful thoughts and emotions. You may find so many benefits in planning meals that you want to apply that organizational tool to other aspects of your life as well.

Physical Benefits

As you chop, dice and mix your ingredients you are also moving your body in beneficial ways, increasing wrist flexibility, loosening joints and improving hand dexterity. Why not turn on some music and have a dance while you cook and really embrace the feel-good factor? It's a great chance to get some light exercise in before you delve into your feast. Try a few quick arm curls with your squash before you chop it up, squat to pick up your potatoes from the sack and lift your pumpkin above your head. Have some fun in the kitchen and pump up the volume.

Mental Health Benefits

You might be busy following a recipe or panicking at timing everything right, but take a breath, hold on to the moment as your home-grown produce is around you and the appetizing smells start to fill the kitchen. Try the wellbeing tips on page 150 as you cook and eat, to fully immerse yourself in the moment for a more fulfilling cooking experience.

No-waste harvest gluts

There will inevitably be times as you grow your own food when you'll discover the harvest glut. Your squash plants might produce more than anticipated and your cabbages may have an immense year. You will need to factor in time to harvest, wash, store, cook and freeze your delicious produce. There are loads of ways to ensure nothing gets wasted and you can enjoy all of the nutrients in each and every fruit and vegetable that you've grown.

Pickles, chutneys and sauces

The go-to for courgettes, apples, runner beans, chillies, tomatoes and just about anything else you can mush up! It's a great way of using a large quantity of ingredients. Chop it all up, chuck it in a saucepan, add the sugar and spices specified in your recipe, and your home will be filled with amazing smells of home cooking.

Fermenting

For a pot of probiotic goodness, fermenting is an age-old technique for storing food. The natural process converts carbohydrates into alcohol or acids, which in turn preserve the food and give it a really distinct flavour. There are fermenting recipes for beans, cauliflower and cucumber, and making sauerkraut is an easy way to use up cabbage. It's simple, quick and good for you.

Drying and dehydrating

Another way to ensure your fruit and vegetables don't go to waste is to dry them in the oven, microwave or a dehydrator. Make apple crisps by slicing apples thinly, placing them well spread apart on a baking sheet and sprinkling with cinnamon. Bake them in the oven for about an hour at 110°C (225°F, Gas Mark ¼) and you have your very own baked apple crisps! Cherries, pears, mushrooms and tomatoes can all be dried for storing.

AS YOU COOK

When possible, take a moment to stop what you are doing. Look around and feel gratitude for the food you are making. Really 'taste' your experience in all ways (not just when you sample the food as it cooks), from the colours of the fresh produce to the aromas of the kitchen. Acknowledge that patience learnt in the garden can be transferred to the kitchen as well for stress-free culinary enjoyment.

AS YOU EAT

Numerous studies have shown how important social connection is to our wellbeing, so share your culinary expertise with friends and family for a delicious boost to your happiness. Your meal, full of home-grown goodness, will be the talk of the table, bolstering your confidence and filling you with pride. Whether you've made a chocolate beetroot cake for a party or rustled up a buffet for your favourite people, revel in the fact you made it all happen from a tiny seed in your hand.

AFTER THE MEAL

Enjoy the affinity you have with both your plants and your guests as you observe everyone coming together. Whether it's a meal for two or a party for a group, these relationships are important. Take a moment after eating to check in with how you feel: do you feel that you belong? Are you enriched? Do you feel optimistic? Accomplished? Remember these emotions. Be proud and leave the clearing up to someone else!

Flowers as Food

Plants will never fail to surprise you. As they bloom and grow, there will be times when you simply take moments to marvel at their beauty. There is more to flowers than aesthetics though. Many are used in cooking, cosmetics and medications, providing incredible health and nutritional benefits. Even some plants that we definitely wouldn't pick and eat ourselves are used in controlled circumstances in prescribed medication, such as foxgloves (*Digitalis*), which are poisonous to eat but are used to treat some heart conditions, and daffodils (*Narcissus*), another toxic plant, that has been found to slow progression of Alzheimer's disease.

As you take in the wonderful world of plants, have a look to see which flowers in your garden are also

edible. Start by researching what you are already growing and what you are planning to grow in the future. If you would like to include more edible flowers in your patch, consider what you will use them for. Will you use them as a garnish, in a fancy cocktail or for cake decorating? When you consider what you might use them for, you can decide what best to grow.

Popular Edible Flowers

Nasturtiums (*Tropaeolum majus*). The foliage, flowers and seed pods are all edible. The brightly coloured flowers in red, orange and yellow jazz up a salad with a mild peppery flavour. You can also pickle the seed pods as an alternative to capers.

Pansies (*Viola × wittrockiana*). With so many colours to choose from and all being edible, they are often used as colourful cake decorations, as they adhere easily to icing. They also have antioxidant and anti-inflammatory properties. When you pick the flowers this will stimulate more growth, meaning even more to eat.

Snapdragons (*Antirrhinum*). They aren't the most flavoursome edible flowers but they do look fabulous perched on a cocktail glass! Crystallize them for extra pizzazz by rinsing and fully drying, then coating with a little syrup (use maple syrup or a sugar and water mix) and sprinkling with a little caster sugar. Let them dry overnight and your guests will be amazed.

Cornflower (*Centaurea cyanus*). The flowers have a gentle spicy flavour with a dash of sweetness as well. If you want to brighten up a salad, blue, red and pink cornflowers look spectacular. You can also bake them in cookies and focaccia.

Surprising Edible Flowers

Dahlias have become incredibly popular due to the many colours, shapes and sizes available to grow. There is a dahlia or ten for every garden! You can peel and steam or boil the tubers, although the flavour varies depending on the variety, and the stunning flowers look spectacular atop cakes and other dishes.

Fuchsia. The little ballerina flowers are all edible and look incredible in jellies and trifles. If you collect lots of the berries they can be made into jam.

Hawthorn (*Crataegus monogyna*). The little white buds in early spring and red berries later in the year are both edible. Harvesting a few will be enough to taste the slight coconut flavour from the flowers, which are perfect for garnishes. You can also dry the fruit to sprinkle on your cereal in the mornings.

Daylilies (*Hemerocallis*). While each flower only blooms for one day, they do continue to flower for weeks and have bright, cheerful flowers. Every part of the daylily is edible, but it is the flower buds that provide the real treat. Pick them before they open, dip them in batter and fry them. Have some hummus ready to dip them into and enjoy the tasty feast.

Enjoy every moment of growing, harvesting and being creative with edible flowers. It can bring so much sparkle to your cooking and add to your appreciation of the multiple benefits of plants.

> **EAT EDIBLE FLOWERS** in moderation. It's a good idea to start in small quantities first, after checking it is safe to do so for you. Always make sure there are no contraindications with your own allergies or medicines.

Sharing is Caring

The beauty of gardening is that you can garden alone and enjoy being by yourself, listening to the birds and the bees as you tend to your plants, but you can also open up your garden and share your new knowledge and experiences with your neighbours, friends, family and the wider community.

By helping when we can, sharing what we have grown and being caring towards others, we may also feel fulfilled and better connected. Supportive, strong and nourishing relationships will help you find contentment. Not only that,

but when you share, you could be changing someone else's world too. Showing that you care is a great strength – it's also a valuable way to make the world a better place and create opportunities for the future.

Ways You Can Share and Care

Whether you are keen to share your garden with friends and family or you're looking to support the wider community, here are some ideas to try:

FRIENDS AND FAMILY

Showing your passion for what you have learnt and achieved will be infectious and you might even encourage your friends to start gardening too. Another way to share your love for the garden is to give some of it away.

Herbs are particularly great for gifting: simply snip off the stems and bunch together with a piece of string. To keep them fresh put some damp kitchen paper around the bottom of the cut stems. They will look pretty, smell divine and your friends can cook with them or propagate them.

Cut flowers are full of beauty and simple to snip, tie together and give to someone as a thank you, a pick-me-up – or simply just because. You can use flowers to make decorative seasonal wreaths, pop some in a bucket of water and leave on someone's doorstep as a surprise, or go all out and create a stunning posy for a friend. No matter what you share, big or small, the thought will be appreciated and sometimes the little things are even more impactful.

Fruit and vegetable sharing is a gift within a gift! It's not just the thought but also the nutritional benefit and fun your friends and family will get from cooking the produce you have grown. Why not bag up what you want to share and pop in a handwritten copy of your favourite recipe?

Cooking is another way to share what you have grown. Invite a friend or a group of friends to chat, laugh, talk about the food you've made and to share your gardening stories with.

Cuttings, seeds and divisions are wonderful ways to share your garden plants with others. Collect seeds from your plants and pack them into paper bags labelled with the name of the plant and instructions for growing and gift them to friends and family. If you have overgrown perennials that need to be divided, pot a division and pass it on. Your garden can be shared far and wide and bring happiness to many others.

COMMUNITY AND VOLUNTEERING

Finding local projects that need help provides not only an opportunity to meet and learn from neighbours but also for you to share your experience. Volunteering can help build self-confidence as you share your skills in a valued way, at the same time as discovering new friendships.

Have a think about what kind of skills you would like to share. Would you like to contribute to physical gardening

The magic of microgreens

Microgreens are the seedlings of many salads, vegetables and herbs, grown to about 10cm (4in) high before harvesting. They are ideal to use as garnishes for soups, smoothies and salads and in sandwiches for a burst of extra nutrition. They can be grown at any time of year in almost any space where there is light and enough warmth for germination. A bright windowsill is perfect during winter and in a greenhouse or outside during the warmer months. They are so full of nutrition, surprisingly even more than the fully matured vegetable.

How to grow
Sprinkle seeds onto a tray of compost (any will do as long as there are no weeds) and cover with a very fine, thin layer of compost which you will need to keep moist, ideally with a mist sprayer so the soil doesn't get too wet.

tasks where help is required? Can you give some time to help teach the community about gardening? Does your local community garden need homemade cake donations that you can use your courgette glut to make and top with some edible flowers freshly picked from your garden?

There are other ways to share with the community: you could try gardening book clubs, seed swaps with friends, gardening groups or online contacts, and produce

You can also plant the seeds in recycled food pots and tin cans. You can even paint a face on the pot or can as the microgreens will look like hair on top!

Pick from seeds such as broccoli, rocket, sprouts, cress, beetroot, coriander, peas, fenugreek, basil, lettuce, pak choi, radish...the list is long.

Harvesting

Microgreens will be ready to harvest just one to three weeks after sowing, depending on what you are growing. All you will need is some scissors to cut the microgreens when they have developed a few sets of leaves and grown no taller than 10cm (4in). If you leave part of the stem in the soil you will get a shorter second harvest after which you can replenish the soil and start over again.

exchanges at your allotments or community garden groups. Find out if your local food bank will accept homegrown food, deliver flowers to a nursing home or leave garden treats on neighbours' doorsteps. You really can make someone's day.

Environmental Impact

Sharing isn't just about giving things to other people and time to community projects, it is also about recognizing how much you already share with the natural world. Each flower you grow is being shared with others – from the person who walks by and admires it with a smile, to the bee that drinks the nectar and buzzes off to pollinate your crops. Your garden is shared by thousands of insects that are equally busily sharing their work with you, even though you can't see it all happening. You are part of the ecosystem as you provide and care for your garden. You are sharing the trees, the landscape and the air that you breathe with all living creatures on this planet. We share every moment of our interconnected lives in one way or another and, as you garden, know that what you are tending to is creating a positive, uplifting, beneficial environment to share with generations to come.

Starting Again

Your garden throughout the year has been a place of refuge, where you have spent time thinking, forgetting, focusing, meditating and working to make a positive impact. You will have made connections to the natural world in ways that have enlightened and fascinated you. This intrinsic connection to our wellbeing brings compassion, empathy and huge appreciation for life on this planet.

From worms in the soil to blackbirds in the trees, each and everything is linked. As you observe the seasons you'll see that most of the garden sleeps in winter and you'll be amazed at the extraordinary regrowth in spring as the biological life cycle continues in your garden.

Keeping a thriving garden requires observation and work all year, but there are certain times when you will notice more clearly how the cycle starts over again. Watching the process closely can teach us many valuable lessons. Fear of failure can stop us in our tracks but observing our gardens teaches us that we should never be afraid to start all over again. The best part of starting over is that you've learnt valuable lessons along the way that you can use next time around. Just as plants have evolved, adapting to changes and tough conditions, you can too. Gardening can help you to accept that sometimes things don't work out but you can find the persistence and desire to try again.

> **LIFE LESSONS** Starting over is not a failure – it is building on what you already have and, importantly, it shows resilience, strength, tenacity, bravery and a positive attitude to keep striving for your goals.

In the garden you will be starting over almost every step of the way. When you harvest your cut-and-come-again salads the new growth will start again; when you lift your dahlia tubers in autumn and tuck them away for winter, the cycle has begun again; when you add mulch to the soil, you are reinvigorating it, ready to start growing again.

There will be specific times in the garden when you will need to start afresh, as a process of renewal and ongoing; the following are just some of these:

A Full Revamp

A blank canvas or the decision to completely remodel your garden is the ultimate way to begin a new journey, giving yourself a completely clean start to pave the way to brighter things. When you decide to undertake such an adventure, make it not just a project in the garden but a journey to discovery for yourself.

Composting and Mulching

This garden activity is perhaps the most obvious aspect of starting over. You have grown plants, then removed them for whatever reason to put into the compost heap. You exclude light from the compost, worms help to break the plant material down and you turn the compost occasionally to ensure everything is decomposing and oxygen is available. Over time those old plants turn into compost which is then re-applied to the soil. Then in following seasons, the same cycle will happen again and again.

Sowing and Planting

Each time you sow a seed, you are starting afresh. Every time you plant something new out, you are starting again. Every year you replenish your hanging baskets, pots and containers you are getting another chance to improve, grow and replenish. Likewise, each time you deadhead a

flower, you are allowing another to bloom in its place and when you prune back flowering shrubs, they too will grow and flower again, starting over. Most of the garden dies back in winter, so it can start all over again in spring. Everything has a process of renewal. It teaches us that starting over is completely natural, and in doing so we are provided with new opportunities to flourish and even do it better next time.

Mistakes and Mishaps

Every day is a fresh day and another opportunity to try something new. Gardening teaches us that sometimes things simply don't work out despite our best efforts. Maybe you forgot to water your pots and the plants wilted, perhaps you had a terrible crop of onions or your tomatoes got blight. Things happen, and you can learn from them and move on. In fact, making mistakes in the garden is one of the best ways to find out how not to do something! Every gardener of any level of experience will make mistakes – you are not alone.

Life Lessons in the Garden

Take a look around your garden. Observe the trees, your plants and the wildlife. In a notebook, make a list using the following prompts:

- Write a note of anything that isn't growing so well.
- Make a list of things you would like to change.
- Note down what you will do differently next time.
- Bullet point gardening lessons that you have learnt.

Next to the list from your garden, write a list about your own life.

- What aspects of your life are not as positive as you would like?
- What would you like to change to improve your life and wellbeing?
- Is there anything that you will do different going forward?
- What lessons can you take with you into the future?

When you have your lists, identify one area from your garden and one from your life that you can make beneficial changes to. Make a commitment to those two areas, taking a fresh approach to how you will take these forward positively for the future.

Sometimes it can be a difficult decision to start over but by aligning the changes that you need to make in your life with the changes in your garden, you can approach this in a more positive way, seizing the chance to refresh and rebalance, and, as you watch the seasons change, you will know there are great times ahead for you.

Taking Stock and Reflection

During your year in the garden as you watch changes and learn how things grow, it's really useful to keep a track of what you observe, what you will do differently next year and your favourite moments in the garden. Note-taking is important for reflection and forward planning. It's not all about the garden though. You are on your own journey so don't forget to make notes to help yourself grow too.

WORDS AND SKETCHES

It can be handy to keep a gardening notebook in the shed to use as you go along or perhaps by your bed if you like note-taking before you sleep. Either way, mix it up by including not just notes about your day but also sketches of what you've enjoyed and include how you felt when you were gardening as well. Draw bubble diagrams, flow charts and use different coloured pencils to bring it all to life. Brain dump it all in your notebook which will soon become an important gardening resource. You will find over time that looking back on it will bring so much joy.

GROWTH MINDSET

This adventure with your garden is one where you grow together, and in the process you work out how to tackle obstacles, learn why things haven't turned out as planned and look forward to the future ahead. This will help you establish a growth mindset – not just for your plants. Believe that you can grow and your talents can constantly evolve and flourish. As you write in your notebook, make room for some positive affirmations each day, such as:

'I never give up.'
'I have great ideas.'
'I am growing.'
'I can do anything.'
'I am confident.'
'I am a gardener.'

Capturing the Garden Year with Photos

Photographs provide snapshots of moments in time, mostly the memories of positive, enjoyable and special times in our lives. They allow us to look back with fondness, keeping precious occasions in our minds forever more. Taking snapshots of your garden means you can tell your story and recall each season, year after year.

Looking at your garden through a lens also means you will see things that you haven't noticed before, you can view your plants from angles you might not usually notice and even get much closer in a macro shot, revealing tiny details and providing an even more powerful connection with your plants.

The story of your garden isn't just about the plants, it's about you as well. In time, you will look back and see just how far your own gardening journey has progressed. When you look at your photos you will remember the feelings and emotions you had at the time and you'll be able to share appreciation for your garden with friends and family.

What to Photograph

Your garden will give you endless opportunities to take photos. From the bugs all around to the plants, the sky, wildlife visitors, the grass – everything that makes your garden so special. You can take photos of your pots and containers looking their very best, and even capture the garden at its worst. Get close and capture the finer details, then stand back and get the whole picture – you can snap it all.

We are more likely to take photos of beautiful and interesting things but in order to really document your garden journey, taking photos of the aspects that didn't work can be useful in looking at ways to successfully develop and move forward. Is there a patch that you want to improve? Get it on camera so you won't forget and can look at it and decide what you would like to do to change it. Is there a plant that is struggling? Take a photo and use it to research in books, online or ask for advice from a local gardening club, social media group or even at your local nursery. Finding out the answer and having a plan will make that photo really worth it. When you have improved a spot in the garden, you can compare the before and after photos and celebrate your success.

Ideally, take photos throughout the year so you can compare different months and seasons, see the development of new plants and record family times. It will give you the opportunity to look at the photos during the quieter, colder months when the garden is dormant and to plan for the following year.

Fun with Photos

Printing some photos and keeping them in a place you can easily access will mean you can check them speedily when you want to; storing them in albums on your phone is also useful and a great way to quickly upload them online if needed. But as this part of your journey is a big celebration of what you have achieved, why not have some creative fun and keep a photo journal or scrapbook?

Scrapbooks are so enjoyable to put together. A key advantage of scrapbooking is that you can make space not just for photos but for text describing each one. You can include how you felt at the time in each photo, the date and other details. Leave spaces free so you can stick progression photos in as well over the years. You will be surprised and full of satisfaction when you see this record of how your garden has evolved.

Photo albums are another great idea for holding precious memories. Don't forget to write the date and details underneath each photo so you can recall the month and year of each.

Display photos in your home. Upload photos online to create ready-made photo tiles or print out and place in frames. Another lovely and cheap way to display photos is to hang them from pegs clipped onto a length of string. You can then swap photos out as often as you like.

Photographs are your memories, a way to celebrate your garden and a way to bring happiness.

Time for Reflection

At times throughout your gardening journey you will pause for reflection, most notably at the end of each season and during the quieter months of the year. This time provides you with a chance to recognize how far you have come. As part of reflection, there will be time to show gratitude towards everything you have encountered and to learn more about the wider environment, including essential trees. By immersing yourself in true appreciation and gratitude for the natural world, you will not just experience magical moments in nature but will also discover your true self.

Appreciating Your Work

Appreciation

noun. *'recognition and enjoyment of the good qualities of someone or something'*

Showing kindness and appreciation to others is something that brings us great joy. Self-appreciation, however, is much harder because we are far more critical of our own actions. It's about sending the kindness and generosity that you give to others in the direction of yourself as well. It's about being grateful to you from you, without judgement. Giving yourself gratitude can boost your morale, provide further motivation and can help you to work through tough times, contributing to a better sense of inner peace.

Allow yourself the time and space to take moments in the garden alone so you can feel true connection to the natural world and harness pride and joy at what you have achieved. It doesn't matter how big or small your efforts have been, every single one counts.

When other people show us appreciation it feels good. But we often forget to appreciate just how much we deserve it from ourselves.

Self-appreciation Activity

Practise this exercise to celebrate your achievements in the garden.

1. Put your feet up, grab a warm drink, notebook, pen and a clean jar or a tin.
2. Start to reflect on your year and all of the achievements you've had in the garden.
3. For everything you think of that didn't work out, think of two positive things you achieved.
4. Write each positive thing you achieved on a separate piece of paper, also noting down how you made it happen.
5. Put each achievement note into your jar or tin.
6. When you have finished, go for a walk in the garden and reinforce the positive achievements by thanking yourself out loud (or in your head if you prefer).
7. If you have times when you are struggling to appreciate yourself, take out an achievement note from the jar or tin and read it to yourself.

This is an activity you can do for many aspects of your life. Remember that compassion and forgiveness are not just for you to give to others. It's important to also express these to yourself.

Show Gratitude to Your Garden

Your garden is alive, even when you think it isn't: even if your borders are bare and your grass is patchy, there is so much life around you; even in the depths of winter, the garden is a hive of activity beneath the soil. Plants, trees and wildlife continue to work doing their very best to make sure the planet's ecosystems survive. How often do you show gratitude directly to the plants, shrubs, trees and wildlife in your garden? They are all working with you to grow a biodiverse space that you can be proud of, where you relax, have fun, where you can just be you.

It is as easy as simply saying 'thank you' to anything that is part of your garden. To the overgrown nettles for the plant feed they become, to the gooseberry bushes that continue to produce fruit year after year that you enjoy in desserts, to the tree that provides shade and shelter for you and birds, to the herbs that nourish your body, the wisteria for its abundance of lilac flowers that make you smile, the blue tits that nest each year in the bird box for the joy they bring when the chicks hatch. There is an abundance to be grateful for in your garden every day of the year, so show your appreciation by saying 'thank you' and nurturing everything to the best of your ability so your garden continues to thrive.

Let Others Appreciate Your Garden

When you garden, there are many skills that you use, most likely without even realizing it. As a gardener you are also a scientist and a naturalist, but you are actually applying geography skills, philosophy, art, maths and much more. You are becoming more multi-talented with every day you step outside and get your hands dirty. You are a considerate neighbour for making your neighbourhood a more beautiful place, and you are a great friend to the natural world.

What you can also be is the person who spreads the word about the rewards and benefits of gardening. One way to do that is to let other people into your garden to appreciate all of your hard work. Not only might it inspire them to try gardening, but you could share knowledge and get gardening tips from other gardeners. When someone appreciates your garden by visiting and enjoying being outside in the space, commenting on the colours, how lovely your flowers are or how pretty the pots look on the patio, they are expressing admiration for everything you have done. It's not just friends and family that you could invite – perhaps consider a coffee morning for neighbours, a charity garden afternoon tea or even an open garden day.

By opening up and sharing and by accepting appreciation for your hard work in the garden, you will also be able to find appreciation for yourself on a much deeper level than ever before.

The Art of Forest Bathing

Forest bathing is known as *shinrin-yoku* in Japan where it's often practised to help reduce blood pressure, stress and anxiety. It's an activity that you don't need your swimwear for, despite the name – it is a simple method of being calm and quiet among trees.

Breathe in the forest scents, marvel at the light beaming through the trees, look up at the canopy and listen intently to the sounds around you and under your

feet. Walking in the trees with intention is an act of self-care, giving you the time to feel revitalized as you breathe life into your lungs.

HOW TO FOREST BATHE

1. Walk slowly and engage all of your senses until you feel relaxed.
2. Take a few minutes to stand or sit with your eyes closed.
3. Declutter your brain and release tension from your muscles.
4. Give yourself time to feel your emotions in the moment.
5. When you open your eyes, look around in awe. What do you see? Is everything more vibrant? Do you see greater detail?
6. Breathe it all in.

FIVE THINGS TO LOOK OUT FOR

1. Marvel at the different shapes and colours of fungi among the trees.
2. Try to identify the trees around you (see page 190).
3. Look out for tiny wildflowers.
4. Spot the woodland birds flying from tree to tree.
5. Hug a tree and whisper a 'thank you' for helping to keep you alive.

When you walk surrounded by trees, you will feel your connection to the wonder of the natural world.

Seasonal Changes

When you nurture a garden, you have a wonderful opportunity to work with and for mother nature. There is no better way to appreciate the importance of seasons than to embrace each one for its distinct beauty and use this as inspiration to celebrate the circle of life.

Wellbeing Throughout the Seasons

Think about the individual benefits that each season brings and, alongside this, consider the activities that you might engage with to make the most of these benefits.

SPRING

When bulbs push their way up through the soil after a winter of hiding away and suddenly erupt in an array of uplifting colours, you can rejoice at the season of new life, renewal and hope. Crocus fill gardens and daffodils grace vases in early spring, then later in the season tulips, bluebells and alliums arrive in all of their glory. Woodland areas wake up, birds sing from the trees as they busily hold territory and build nests. Trees become full of buds and our souls feel lifted with great expectations for the year ahead.

Relish moments to appreciate the seasonal shift by stopping to admire bulbs in fields and on verges, look up at the blue sky and get outside more to absorb some vitamin D. The transformation at this time of year isn't just in the garden, as we also naturally find the spring in our step coming out of winter hibernation. Take some time to look closely at the changes in the world around you and feel your whole mind, body and soul lift to the sounds and sights of spring in your garden.

Activity: collect some spring flowers or blossom for your home as a delightful pick-me-up. Gather a selection of small vases or recycled glass bottles and place one stem in each. Huddle the vases and bottles together for an uplifting display.

SUMMER

With the longer days and warm evenings, summer is the season for outdoor living and lush green growth in the garden, spongy lawns to walk on and an array of rainbow colours in pots and containers. Delphinium, gladioli, echinacea, cosmos and sunflowers will all be flowering their socks off. Spot bees covered in pollen, butterflies bathing on buddleja and ladybirds hiding in the nettles.

Waking up to the warm sun shining through the window is a great way to start the day. Opening the curtains to admire your garden in full bloom will help your confidence

and self-esteem, preparing you for the day ahead. Just looking at your plants can provide a mood boost, so as you water your garden, admire the artistry that nature is providing, with your helping hand. Feel proud as you smell the roses, run your hands through feathery grasses, spot fledglings leave their nests and harvest flowers, fruit and vegetables to nourish your body.

Activity: lie in the garden and let time go by as you feel the sunshine on your skin and drink in all the beauty around you. If you can, tie a hammock between trees and relax into a gentle swing or lie on the grass and look up to the sky. Don't forget your sunscreen!

AUTUMN

Crisp air and tonal transformations across the landscape dominate autumn, providing a chance to watch the move towards the colder months of the year. When seasons change, it reinforces that change is inevitable and happens for a reason. Embrace the seasonal shift by putting your cosy sweater on and wrap your hands around a spiced herbal tea before you get to work on helping your plants make their way through the decreasing temperatures.

In the garden, there will be leaf fall on the ground and perennials that have lost their colour but still provide sensational structure and interest with enchanting seedheads and willowy stems. Maybe you will spot a goldfinch on a thistle feeding on the seeds as you mulch your garden plants or a robin close by as you disturb the soil and insects pop up to the surface. Witnessing the changes in the plants you cherish through this transitional time means you get to see them in a whole different light, as you plant spring bulbs with great hope for the future.

Activity: put your boots on and jump in the autumn leaves. Kick them up as high as you can and scoop leaves in your hands, throwing them up into the air and watching them float back down to the ground before you collect them to make leaf mulch (see page 27). Enjoy letting your inner child out to play.

WINTER

The shorter, darker days are starkly different from previous months, but there is so much beauty in winter, from the sparkle on a frosty lawn to the spiders' webs glistening between plants. Know that your plants are tucked away,

storing their energy for spring and summer. The shorter days can be tough but when you cultivate a garden the work never really stops. There will always be a reason to go outside: your feathered friends need feeding, your pathways may need clearing, shrubs need pruning and when snow falls you can grab your hat, scarf and gloves to build a snowman.

Marvel at the ability of nature to head into dormancy so it can spring back to life the following year. Recognize that sometimes you need to take a rest so you can revitalize yourself as well. Look closely at detail because what you find will be entirely different to what you see when everything is in bloom. Your garden is dynamic and contrasting, providing a different kind of beauty for the eye to see during each and every season. Observe the various patterns, colours, shapes and textures because winter allows you to see the very core of your garden.

Activity: make your own food for your garden birds to help them through the winter. Spread some peanut butter on the outside of a cardboard toilet-roll tube and sprinkle wild bird seed on so it sticks. Then make a couple of holes and tie up outside with string. Don't forget to take photos, capturing the beauty of your own winter wonderland (see Capturing the Garden Year with Photos, pages 168–171).

Fungi foraging

The world of fungi provokes a flurry of fascination and images of fairies perched on toadstools. Fungi expertly break down organic matter and help to transfer nutrients and water from the soil into plant roots – all of which happens without you seeing, so they really can be thought of as magical.

You are most likely to see fungi in woodland as they live on decaying wood. The fun of the forage is in the anticipation of what you will find and even the knowledge that it might be poisonous. *It's imperative to know what you are picking so learn about different species and if they are safe enough to eat before collecting* – you can take photos to identify them at home or download an app. You can also join a fungi-foraging group and be guided as to the safe varieties, learning while meeting new friends. If you are unsure, leave it in the ground to continue its essential task of keeping the ecosystem alive. To harvest edible fungi, cut the mushrooms near the bottom of the stem, don't pull them up.

Enjoy everything about the forage from the excitement when finding something new to listening to the trees rustling in the breeze.

Top Ten Seasonal Jobs in the Garden

You'll find many jobs to do in the garden all year round, so focus on these top ten key tasks for each season.

SPRING

1. Sow seeds such as lettuce, radish, chard, beetroot, nasturtiums (*Tropaeolum majus*), calendula, cosmos.
2. Start mowing the lawn on a high setting.
3. Mulch garden borders, trees and shrubs.
4. Plant out dahlias after the last frost.
5. Start to feed your plants to promote growth.
6. Cut back old hellebore leaves so that you can see the flowers.
7. Deadhead spring bulbs, leaving the foliage to die back.
8. Start weeding as and when needed.
9. Top dress containers with a fresh layer of compost.
10. Plan a watering schedule for your garden.

SUMMER

1. Plant out your summer bedding and hanging basket plants.
2. Keep on top of deadheading to encourage more flowers.
3. Ensure your pots and containers don't dry out.
4. Keep a look out for pests and diseases.
5. Transplant hardened-off plants into their final growing position.
6. Add supports for climbing plants before they get too big.

7. Cover fruit with netting to protect them from birds getting to them first.
8. Add shade to your greenhouse and open vents and doors.
9. Cut back herbs for a second flush before the end of summer.
10. Continue picking your sweet peas (*Lathyrus odoratus*) so they produce more flowers.

AUTUMN

1. Collect leaves to make leaf mulch (see page 27).
2. Plant bare-root perennials such as roses, peonies, delphiniums and rudbeckia.
3. Rejuvenate your pots and containers with winter bedding plants such as cyclamen, heather (*Calluna*) and pansies (*Viola × wittrockiana*).

4. Put containers up on bricks or pot feet to improve drainage.
5. Mulch beds to protect plants from frost and replenish the soil.
6. Clean your greenhouse to stop bugs overwintering.
7. Lift and store or heavily mulch your dahlias.
8. Plant and move shrubs, hedges and trees.
9. Plant garlic, onion and shallot sets to overwinter for an early harvest.
10. Plant your spring bulbs such as daffodil (*Narcissus*), crocus, tulip, hyacinth and allium.

WINTER

1. Clean and tidy inside your shed.
2. Browse seed catalogues to choose next spring's plants.
3. Remove frozen water in bird baths and top up with fresh water.
4. Top up bird feeders every day.
5. Check on pots and containers, scraping snow off if heavy.
6. Enjoy reading some gardening books for education.
7. Collect natural materials to make Christmas decorations.
8. Make new raised beds in preparation for the following spring.
9. Add bubble wrap or other insulation inside your greenhouse to protect plants.
10. Clear out leaf fall in guttering to allow water to flow into your water butts.

Trees
for Life

Watching the sunlight filter through trees is just like seeing a light at the end of the tunnel. Nature truly is a beacon of hope during darker days and being surrounded by trees can give a true sense of connection to greater things, just when you might need it most. Trees have an almost mystical appearance with their silhouettes against the landscape and their whispers through the air as the breeze meets the leaves.

Take some time out and get to know your local trees. Not only will you be stepping out into the fresh air and exercising but you can also get up close to the trees that line your street, local park or woodland. Identifying trees can be good fun, and you will be looking closely at the leaves and bark, giving yourself time to focus, breathe and reduce stress.

How to Identify Trees

Collect a leaf from a tree and look at the shape, details, colours and texture. That leaf is the key to identifying the tree. Needles, scales and broadleaf are the three basic types of leaves to look out for, but you can also identify a tree by its bark, overall shape, flowers and fruit. There are many resources online to help you identify trees.

Drawing. If you fancy sketching what you see, put pencil to paper and draw the shape of the leaf, the leaf pattern and details, the overall tree shape and the bark pattern so you can take it home and do some research. You could even embellish your sketch with colour and background scenery to enjoy as a keepsake.

Tree collages. Try making a fun collage by collecting leaves with various tones and textures. You can create shapes, animals, people or just place them however pleases you. Use a little glue to stick them to paper and identify the trees that they came from as you go along.

Bark rubbing helps you to really appreciate the detail. Feel every bump and groove as you place a piece of paper over the bark and begin to rub with a pencil or crayon onto it. The bark pattern will soon appear on the paper. Don't forget to stick a leaf to the paper as well to help with identification.

Benefits to Us and the Environment

Trees are often described as the 'lungs of the Earth' and it's easy to understand why: they turn the carbon dioxide that we breathe out into the oxygen that we breathe in. Tree roots help to hold soil together, which helps to stop soil erosion, and they contribute to rainfall by taking water from the ground and releasing it into the atmosphere; so, fewer trees means less oxygen, less soil and less rainfall. They also filter pollution, noise, solar rays, dust and wind – they are nature's machines of the land.

TAKE A MOMENT TO BREATHE When you are next breathing in and out deeply, in a moment of mediation or practising a wellbeing activity, close your eyes and focus on *feeling* your breath. Concentrate on how the air feels as it enters and leaves your body. Feel your lungs expand as you literally breathe life into your body and express gratitude to the role our majestic trees play in providing the very air that we breathe.

Supporting Wildlife

When you look at a tree, what do you see? Some of the most mature trees, such as a spectacular oak in the local park, will be a home to thousands of creatures. They are like the most environmentally friendly apartment block! Within the tree there are mosaics of microhabitats, each intertwined in complex ways that contribute to biodiversity. Over the lifetime of a tree the branches, leaves, roots, decaying and hollow wood will be home to birds, insects, fascinating fungi and lichen. Each tree is a true powerhouse for life.

Trees in Your Garden

There are so many tree species suitable for growing in gardens, all dependent on the growth rate and size at maturity, building and neighbouring boundaries and requirements such as sun and moisture. It can seem a difficult choice but a great way to work out what trees might be good for your garden, is to start looking at your neighbours' trees. This will help to give you clues as to what grows well in your area and you might spot a tree that you love. So, take a walk and chat with your neighbours to find out what species grow well in your area. Invest some time in research; not only

will you learn much about our beloved trees, but you might find one that truly blows your mind with its beauty and that will become a garden friend for life.

Think about how your tree will support your garden; are there specific birds you would like to encourage or are you more interested in colourful flowers? Make a list of everything you would love your tree to be so that you can search in a targeted way. Some trees that work well for garden spaces are:

Chinese redbud (*Cercis chinensis* 'Avondale'). This has wonderfully vibrant pink flowers that grow from the branches even before the foliage appears a few weeks later. Growing to only 2.5m (8ft) high, it can also be grown in a large container.

Pink Juneberry (*Amelanchier* × *grandiflora* 'Robin Hill'). With berries for birds and leaves that look spectacular in autumn, it will grow to about 4m (13ft) high and delight you with pale pink buds that open up into pretty white flowers during spring.

Small-space trees

Gardening in a smaller area, or even in pots, needn't stop you from pursuing your dream of growing trees. There are many truly magnificent trees that can grace your small space and provide you with structure, height and all-year interest for you and garden wildlife.

Small-garden trees
- Strawberry tree (*Arbutus unedo*)
- Crab apple (*Malus* 'John Downie')
- Paperbark maple (*Acer griseum*)
- Dogwood (*Cornus kousa* 'Wolf Eyes')
- Star magnolia (*Magnolia stellata* 'Jane Platt')

Trees for containers
- Edible fig (*Ficus carica*)
- Pink silk tree (*Albizia julibrissin* 'Rosea')
- Olive (*Olea europaea*)
- White spruce (*Picea glauca var. albertiana* 'J. W. Daisy's White')
- Dwarf lilac tree (*Syringa meyeri* 'Palibin')

Silver birch (*Betula pendula*). The white bark is a stunning feature of the silver birch and that's even without the glorious bright green leaves, brownish catkins and yellow autumnal leaves before they float to the ground, leaving a willowy silhouette on the landscape.

Common elder (*Sambucus nigra* 'Black Lace'). The fragrant flowers provide nectar for bees and the stunning dark purple berries are loved by birds. The foliage is almost black and turns red in autumn. With a height of 3m (10ft), it is incredibly easy to grow.

Rowan (*Sorbus aucuparia*). Mostly known for the bright red autumn berries, the rowan can grow up to 15m (49ft) high. It has clusters of creamy flowers and pretty, toothed foliage and the berries make a delicious jam.

How to Plant a Tree

Growing trees in containers is straightforward and rewarding. Plant in a pot with drainage full of loamy soil and big enough for the rootball. Some species such as acer and rhododendron will prefer ericaceous compost (see Know Your Compost, pages 58–9). Smaller trees will need to be potted in a smaller pot and then gradually potted up as they grow in size. Replace the top few inches of soil each year and use an organic plant feed to keep it healthy. Pots dry out quickly, especially in the summer, so keep it watered as required.

To plant a tree out in your garden, dig a square hole no deeper than the rootball but two times wider and loosen the soil around the hole with a fork to help roots establish. Water the rootball before planting in the hole, then backfill with soil. Most trees will need to be staked to minimize movement as they establish; use a wooden stake no bigger than one-third of the tree height and use tree ties to secure it to the tree. Water in well and mulch, starting about 10cm (4in) away from the stem.

The most important thing to remember is to water your newly planted tree, in the ground or in a container, routinely for the first couple of years or it may struggle to survive as it establishes. The top soil may seem moist but that water needs to reach the roots, so water thoroughly to ensure the roots are able to absorb what the tree needs to grow.

Every step of planting a tree is planting for the future. It's a precious, deep-rooted and enduring contribution to the planet, so cherish every moment.

When you are out in the woodland or around your trees in the garden, take a moment to have a tree hug! There is much mythology surrounding trees including being symbols of hope, peace, renewal, fertility and love. Your favourite tree will keep your secrets, welcome your company and be there for you when you need to just sit and ponder. A tree is, after all, a friend for life.

Focused Moments

Gardening grounds us – we can escape our busy thoughts, come back into our bodies and awaken our senses. As we occupy ourselves growing plants, we are allowing time to focus on a task with a real purpose that provides such joy, teaches patience and persistence and brings great satisfaction. Focusing intimately on cultivating life, even in small doses, will help you to feel more fulfilled and ease the stress in your mind.

Be in the Present

We cannot change the past or know what the future holds, yet we spend a great deal of time thinking about both. Being in the present moment allows us to focus on what is important and that is the 'now'. Allowing yourself time to do this as you garden can help to relieve stress and anxiety and calm your mind.

Next time you are potting a plant, feel the compost between your fingers and intently focus on your breathing as you bring yourself into the moment. Let every other thought slip away as you wholly focus in on this one moment in time. This can be practised with many gardening activities such as seed sowing and weeding. In fact, you will find, in time, it will happen quite naturally without even trying.

Stop for a Moment

Finding meaning in the little things can help us to shift focus from negativity to finding pleasure and positivity in small, joyful moments. Next time you are in the garden, stop and focus on one individual plant, bird, insect or leaf. Observe its movement, the colour, texture, pattern and consider what purpose it has. As you focus, you will feel your body relaxing and your interest in the object of your focus intensify. You may see so much more than you have before.

End Notes

p25, Soil Life for Connectivity

1 *Earthing: The Most Important Health Discovery Ever!* by Clinton Ober, Stephen Sinatra, Martin Zucker, Basic Health Publications Inc, 2010, 2014.
2 'Healthy Stress-busting Fat Found Hidden in Dirt', *Science Daily*, 29 May 2019, https://www.sciencedaily.com/releases/2019/05/190529094003.htm

p47, Encouraging Biodiversity

3 'Pollinators show flower colour preferences but flowers with similar colours do not attract similar pollinators', *Annals of Botany*, August 2016, https://www.ncbi.nlm.nih.gov/pmc/articles/PMC4970366/

p54, Sowing Seeds for Serenity

4 'Identification of an Immune-Responsive Mesolimbocortical Serotonergic System: Potential Role in Regulation of Emotional Behavior,' by Christopher Lowry et al., *Neuroscience*, (11 May 2007).

p67, Finding Hope in New Growth

5 'Multitasking: Switching Costs', American Psychological Association, (20 March 2006), https://www.apa.org/research/action/multitask

p120, Making the Most of Your Lawn
6 'How to look after your mental health using exercise',
Mental Health Foundation, https://www.mentalhealth.org.
uk/publications/how-to-using-exercise

p128, Letting Nature Find Its Own Way
7 'Ants May Boost CO2 Absorption Enough to Slow
Global Warming', *Scientific American*, https://www.
scientificamerican.com/article/ants-may-boost-co2-
absorption-enough-to-slow-global-warming/

Further Reading

Charles Dowding, Stephanie Hafferty, *No Dig Organic Home & Garden: Grow, Cook, Use & Store Your Harvest* (Permanent Publications, 2017).

Dr Carol Dweck, *Mindset: Changing the Way You Think to Fulfil Your Potential* (Robinson, 2017).

Héctor García, Francesc Miralles, *Forest Bathing: The Rejuvenating Practice of Shinrin Yoku* (Tuttle Publishing, 2020).

Dave Goulson, *The Garden Jungle or Gardening to Save the Planet* (Vintage, 2020).

Professor Alistair Griffiths, Matt Keightley, *RHS Your Wellbeing Garden: How to Make Your Garden Good for You* (London: DK Publishing, 2020).

Sue Stuart-Smith, *The Well-Gardened Mind: The Restorative Power of Nature* (Scribner Book Company, 2021).

Kim Walker, Vicky Chown, *The Handmade Apothecary: Healing Herbal Remedies* (Kyle Books, 2017).

Jack Wallington, *Wild About Weeds: Garden Design with Rebel Plants* (London: Laurence King Publishing, 2019).

Index

Acknowledgements

Thanks to everyone on the Greenfinch Books team who made this such a great experience. Special thanks to Philippa Wilkinson for being a wonderful editorial guide, and Julia Shone for making everything come together. Tokiko Morishima and Romy Palstra for designing the book to perfection and bringing life to the pages.

My agent Charlotte Merritt from Andrew Nurnberg Associates International Ltd who has been a great source of advice and support from the beginning of this journey.

To my husband who has infinite patience and undying support for every idea and adventure that I dream of. Thank you for always encouraging those dreams to come true and for being my sounding board for this book.